The Entry of Henry II

Into Paris, 1549

medieval & renaissance texts & studies

VOLUME 7

This is the second volume of
"Renaissance Triumphs and Magnificences"
New Series

General Editor
Margaret M. McGowan

The Entry of Henri II into Paris
16 June 1549

With an Introduction and Notes

BY

I. D. McFarlane

medieval & Renaissance texts & studies
Center for Medieval & Early Renaissance Studies
Binghamton, New York
1982

*The British Academy has generously assisted
in meeting the publication costs of this book.*

© Copyright 1982

Center for Medieval and Early Renaissance Studies
State University of New York at Binghamton
Binghamton, New York

Library of Congress Cataloging in Publication Data

Main entry under title:

The Entry of Henri II into Paris, 1549.

    (Medieval & Renaissance texts & studies; 7)
    Bibliography: pp. 83–94.
    1. Henry II, King of Frances, 1519–1559.
2. Catherine de Médicis, Queen, consort of Henry II,
King of France, 1519–1589. I. McFarlane, I. D. (Ian
Dalrymple). II. Series.
DC114.3.E63   944'.028 [B]   81–18925
ISBN 0-86698-013-X   AACR2

Printed in the United States of America

Table of Contents

Foreword

This edition of the *livret* of the Paris Entry, 1549, was accepted for publication some years ago; it lay in the original publisher's drawer for a considerable time, and I am very grateful to Professor Mario A. Di Cesare for his willingness to publish the work in the SUNY Binghamton series. In any case, it is an ill wind that blows nobody any good; and delay has meant that I have been able to profit from research recently brought to fruition. By formation, I am more interested in the history of cultural phenomena; but the appearance of work on the social and political background of Royal Entries has allowed me to take a broader view. My Introduction has thus benefited greatly from American colleagues who have been good enough to read my text when it was submitted to the Center for Medieval and Early Renaissance Studies. Some of these remain anonymous; but I am particularly grateful to Professor Ralph E. Giesey, and to his pupil Professor Lawrence M. Bryant who has been generous enough to let me consult his doctoral thesis on French Royal Entries and to use some of his findings in my revised Introduction, which given its limited size has not been able to exploit all the material he has assembled; and readers are advised to consult his dissertation themselves.

I am much indebted to the Keeper of the Bibliothèque Municipale, Toulouse, for permission to use that Library's copy of the *livret* and to reproduce it here; also to Bodley's Librarian, Oxford, for permission to reproduce the copy of the Queen's *Sacre*. Professor Georges Soubeille has been kind enough to help me on various matters, and I owe special thanks to Professor Margaret McGowan, General Editor of the Series as well as to Professor Mario Di Cesare, who have encouraged me to pursue my work on the Entry and have done so much to ensure its publication. Dr. Terence Cave was also kind enough to look at the typescript and offer valuable comment.

Introduction

Abbreviations

I. Libraries

AN	Archives Nationales, Paris
BL	British Library, London
BN	Bibliothèque Nationale, Paris
CUL	Cambridge University Library
FW	Folger Shakespeare Library, Washington
NLS	National Library of Scotland, Edinburgh
OB	Bodleian Library, Oxford

II. Documents and works mentioned frequently in the Introduction:

Belleforest   N. Gilles, D. Sauvage, F. de Belleforest, G. Chappuy. *Les Chroniques et annales de France dès l'origine des François & leurs venues ès Gaules*, 1600.

Bryant   Lawrence M. Bryant. "The French Royal Entry Ceremonial: politics, art and society in Renaissance Paris." Ph.D. dissertation, University of Iowa, 1978.

Bulaeus   Bulaeus (E. du Boulay). *Historia Universitatis Parisiensis*, 6 vols., 1665–73.

BW   O. Bloch & W. von Wartburg. *Dictionnaire étymologique de la langue française*, 5th ed., 1968.

C (or   Accounts of the festivities drawn up by Philippe
Comptes)   Macé for the Municipality, preserved in AN, KK 286A.

Corrozet   Corrozet, G. *Les Antiquitez, croniques et singularitez de Paris, Ville capitale du Royaume de France . . .* , 1586.

Crévier	Crévier, J. B. L. *Histoire de l'Université de Paris depuis son origine jusqu'en l'année 1600*, 7 vols., 1761.
D	Dauzat, A. *Dictionnaire étymologique de la langue française*, 1st ed. 1938, 2nd ed. 1954.
Félibien	Félibien, P. *Histoire de la Ville de Paris*, 5 vols., 1725.
God.	F. Godefroy. *Cérémonial de France*, 2 vols. 1641.
Paradin, Claude	Claude Paradin. *Les Devises heroïques*, Lyon, 1571.
Paradin, G.	G. Paradin. *Histoire de nostre temps* . . . , 1555.
R (or Registres)	P. Guérin. *Registre des déliberations du bureau de la ville de Paris*, III, 1886.
Stewart	John Stewart. *De aduentu Henrici Valesii Christianissimi Francorum Regis in Metropolim Regni Sui Lutetiam Parisiorum oratio habita* . . . *in gymnasio Prelleorum*, Paris, 1549.
STFM	Société des Textes Français Modernes.
Tervarent	G. de Tervarent. *Attributs et symboles dans l'art profane 1450–1600. Dictionnaire d'un langage perdu*, Geneva, 1968.

III. Currency

d	denier
l	livre
s	sol
t	tournois

A. Prelude

(1) 1547–1549: The *Sacre* — Entry into Rheims — Difficulties and Delays

(a) The *Sacre*

To judge by contemporary accounts, the Entry of 1549 into Paris was unparalleled in splendor and stylistic originality. Gilles Corrozet described it as "la plus riche & magnifique qui fut iamais veüe entre les François,"[1] and Guillaume Paradin, in his brief but hyperbolic report, wrote:

> . . . car il sembloit que toute la Gaule se fust arrachée de ses fondemens pour assister & estre participante des congratulations de ce tant heureux & ioyeux aduenement, que tous les bons esprits eussent espuisé leurs belles & ingenieuses inuentions . . . les nobles Parisiens estimoient tout exces estre trop peu en leur endroict contans toute grande despense pour grand proufit, ce qu'ilz ont déclaré par tant de excellentes beautez de toutes choses, quil sembloit que lair, & le monde en fussent embelliz: desquelles en vouloir particulier catalogue ce seroit vouloir inuentorier le promptuaire de toute l'antiquité.[2]

Once allowance is made for the usual exaggeration, the fact remains that the Parisians were deeply impressed by the ceremonial established for the Royal Entry. They had to wait some considerable time for the occasion. On Easter Sunday, 3 April 1547, the King had been welcomed by the Prévôt des Marchands and other officials: he had received them courteously and the Connétable — Anne de Montmorency — had informed them that he

> entendoit faire la plus grande pompe et magnificence, tant ès obsèques et enterrement du feu Roy,[3] son père, et messeigneurs ses deux frères, que aussi à son entrée, et aussi à l'entrée de la Royne, et qu'il ne voulloit que riens y feust espargné, et que, à ceste cause, lesd. Prevost des Marchans et Eschevins advisassent

de faire dresser leurs preparatifz pour y faire leur devoir, qui sera
exemple aux autres villes.   (R, 78–79)

In response to the two letters sent on the King's behalf by Clausse and
Montmorency on 12 April, the City agreed at the Council sessions of
19 and 21 April

quant aux joyeuses entrées du Roy et de la Royne, y aller en la
plus grande triumphe qu'il sera possible . . .   (R, 81)

They set out in some detail the costumes to be worn by the participants
and especially the Enfants de Paris; it was also resolved that

on fera de beaulx eschauffaulx et misteres ès portes Sainct Denis,
le Ponceau et autres lieux acoustumez, et pour ce faire, seront
mandez painctres, inventeurs et gens de bon esperit, pour com-
poser et adviser ausdictz misteres.   (R, 82)

This all suggests a greater adherence to tradition than was to be envisaged later. However, these arrangements bore no immediate fruit,
for reasons that will soon become apparent, and after the ceremonies at
Rheims there was to be a delay of nearly two years before Paris could
have its Entry.

On the other hand, the *sacre* and coronation, essential to the continuity of royal authority, took place as early as possible.[4] These
ceremonies are worth looking at, as in several respects they show sharp
differences of emphasis and style with the 1549 Entry. After the
harangue delivered by the chief legal officer of the city, Henri reached
the first city gate, where a stage displayed the Royal arms and others;
and a machine had been constructed representing a "Soleil clos en
forme d'une pomme ronde," within which was a "coeur couleur de
geulle." It contained a nine-year-old girl, who, as the King approached
and the sun opened out, handed him the keys of the city (God. I, 304).
Between this and the second gate was

Vne montagne faite en forme de rocher entr'ouuert, & dans le
creux des Monstres marins, des Syrenes & des Satyrs, representez
par des ieunes hommes enuironnez de lierre & de mousse. Il y
auoit aussi sur la mesme riuiere (mais plus loin) un nauire peint &
azuré auec tous ses attirails, & conduit par des Sauuages, qui
faisoient mille sauts & postures, comme voulans attaquer les
monstres qui gardoient le rocher . . .   (ibid., I, 305)

At the second gate the King was met by the *échevins*, and at the end of the high street he came upon

> Vn Theatre esleué sur trois portes disposées en forme d'Arc de triomphe; ce Theatre estoit soustenu de pilliers iaspez & madrez, sur lesquels estoit une gallerie à grandes colonnes par dessus & au milieu une salle auançant sur la ruë auec six percées d'huisseries à l'antique, remplies de pilliers, & de tous les ornemens de l'Architecture . . .   (ibid., I, 306)

In the gallery were thirteen young persons, one male, the rest female, representing the Virtues whose symbols they bore: thus Hope held "un dard brisé, signifiant l'homme immortel," Obedience a golden beehive standing for a "Republicque bien policée," and so forth. Below, "une table d'attente" listed these Virtues in verse. During the Entry the musicians had assembled under the dome; and when the King passed on his way, he came to a

> Iardin de plaisance basty sur un eschaffaut, où estoit un Lys à trois fleurons, qui portoient chacun un enfant vestu de drap d'argent, & de taffetas. Sur ce Lis paroissoit un Croissant haut esleué, sur lequel estoit un enfant tenant une Couronne d'or en la main, dont il couronna le dit Croissant, chantant auec les autres en Musique . . . Proche du Lys, principale fleur du iardin de plaisance, estoit une fille richement parée, laquelle iettoit abondance de lait par ses mammelles & representoit la Charité Royne des Vertus, par laquelle Dieu mesme a souuent esté figuré par les Anciens.   (ibid., I, 307)

The King proceeded along various streets until he reached the Porte de la Cité which also was decorated with a triumphal arch "garny de festons, de peintures, d'emblesmes, de ses armes, de celles de la Royne, & de Monsieur le Dauphin." Amidst the acclaims of the people, he had time to look at a thirty-six-foot high fountain, from the top of which nymphs poured water from their pitchers on to the street below. Nearby was a tall pillar on which the goddess of Fame stood, also pouring water from her trumpet:

> Contre ce pillier estoient trois Monstres marins faits en forme de leston, tous nuds, & tenant chacun une trompe d'airain d'où sortoit du vin clairet, qui tomboit dans des bassins ouvrez de plusieurs feüillages, & figures, où les Suisses de la Garde du Roy

se rafraischirent au iour de l'Entrée & pendant le Sacre.
(ibid., I, 308)

Once in the precincts of the Cathedral, the King listened to the harangue and, having delivered his own speech before the Portal, entered within. Afterwards, he proceeded to the Archbishop's palace in front of which had been erected a pyramid forty-four feet high and crowned by a "grant Croissant Argenté, & au dessus quatre autres Croissans soustenus de huict gros pilliers iaspez & madrez" (ibid, I, 309). At eight o'clock in the evening, the King returned to the Cathedral, then went back to the Palace to rest until the following day when the *sacre* was due to take place.

The Entry into Rheims shows a transitional character. The triumphal arches were already in evidence at such ceremonies, as were the pyramid and the stress on classical motifs in the architectural designs. Yet more traditional aspects were prominent: the *tableaux vivants*, the allegorical figures more medieval than classical in inspiration (the Virtues), the *jardin de Plaisance*, the fountains that ran wine; the planners of the Paris Entry will make a conscious effort to dispense with these old-world features.

(b) Difficulties and Delays

However, various factors conspired to delay the King's Entry into Paris. Up to a point, he was beset by a host of problems, political and military. The precarious balance of power between Francis I and Charles V of Germany had tilted in favor of the latter after his victory over the Protestants at Mühlberg (24 April 1547); and in Italy the assassination of Farnese and the occupation of Piacenza further weighted the scales to his advantage. Pope Paul III opened negotiations with France, while Henri II sought support in Germany by a secret alliance with Maurice of Saxony. At home, the struggle between the Guise and the Montmorency factions at court was sharpening and leaving its mark on foreign policy. In 1548 Montmorency renewed hostilities with England and sent a force to the help of Marie de Guise, the widow of James V of Scotland; and it was only in 1550 that peace was patched up. There was further trouble at home: the revolt in Guyenne against the *gabelle* was repressed with the utmost severity by Montmorency who treated Bordeaux with special vindictiveness. Religious problems were also to the fore: Henri II had every intention of stamping out heresy wherever it showed itself, and almost immediately after his accession the *chambre ardente* was set up, though it really did not get under way for some years. However, all these problems do not get to the bottom of the delay; the fact is that during the first two years of his reign Henri II effected nearly thirty Entries in the country at large, and one may conclude that, had he so wished, he could have entered his capital city some time before he actually did. This is confirmed by a point that was shrewdly picked up by the observant Spanish ambassador: he noted on 20 November 1547 that the King had refused to confirm the City's privileges, that he hoped to remove from its control a host of offices and that he wished to exact from the citizens a sum of over 300,000 francs. Behind his thinking may also have lain the thought that the City was well enough endowed financially to fortify itself powerfully. By withholding his confirmation of privileges he hoped to extract a greater financial gift from the capital than would otherwise have been the case. Entries would normally involve the confirmation of privileges, or modifications of the current situation as seemed proper at the time.[5]

Still, matters could not be delayed indefinitely, and other considerations had to be taken into account. Contemporaries were agreed that one of the functions of kingship was to be seen: a few years later, Guillaume Paradin wrote:

> Il n'y ha rien, qui tant maintienne un Peuple en obeissance & fidelité, que la veue de son souverain Prince, & naturel Seigneur.[6]

Henri II himself attached great importance to protocol, which seems to have made itself felt at court much more than during Francis I's reign, and he was fully aware of the impact that should be made by formal ceremony. On 22 December 1548 he had ordered the drawing up of a *Recueil des Rangs & Seances* and expressed the wish that these extracts from earlier records

> feront mention speciale de la qualité de l'Assemblée, & si elle estoit solennelle en forme d'Estats, ou d'Entrées des Roys nos antecesseurs en leurs Villes . . . ou autres solennelles Assemblées, esquelles les Rangs & ordres se soient gardez, & assignez à un chacun. (God., I, fol. e iiij)

Henri II cannot have taken much pleasure in the number of Entries recently effected by Philip II, and one may feel that the Paris Entry reflects among other things a desire on the King's part to beat the Emperor at his own game. Nearer home, the city of Lyon had put on a magnificent Entry in 1548, which would hardly be music in the ears of Parisians; and certain features that had been particularly notable will leave their mark on the Paris Entry: the obelisk "taillé à la rustique," the double triumphal arch featuring the Rhône and the Saone, the major presence of classical allegorical figures (e.g. *Occasio*), the *termini* associated with a triumphal arch, certain neo-classical traits (columns, perspective), and of course the *naumachia*. On the other hand, the classical gods were numerous rather than tidily grouped round a few dominant motifs, the classical orders were not exploited so methodically as they were to be in 1549, the quatrains to the Queen were spoken by a series of living allegorical figures; and one might think that, as described in the *livret*, the Lyon Entry had a more explicitly religious flavor. Nevertheless, given the long-established rivalry between the two cities, such a display was bound to sharpen the pride of the capital and to confirm its citizens in their desire to put on the finest show ever.

(II) Preparations for the 1549 Entry

Early in 1549 steps were taken to implement the instructions contained in the letters of 1547; on 16 February the decision was taken by the City fathers to engage artists and various specialists for the preparations. At that time it was expected that the Entry would take place on 15 May. The records hint at some resentment at the King's dilatoriness — understandably[7] — but much thought was given to the ways and means of financing the festivities, and it was agreed that

> on doibt faire toutes les magnifficiences et triumphes qu'il sera possible à l'entrée dud. Seigneur tant en theatres, eschauffaulx, piramides que autres singularitez.   (R, 154)

Early entries in the municipal records relate, as one would expect, to money matters. There are references to the financial situation resulting from the purchase "des places à la Court la Royne, pour mectre l'artillerie d'icelle" (R, 154), and from work undertaken on the new buildings of the Hôtel de Ville and on the Fontaine des Innocents, whose opening was meant to coincide with the royal Entry. It was agreed to make to the Queen a present worth some seven or eight thousand l.t.; but in order to do this, permission had to be obtained from the King to use the "plus valleurs" of the farms of the Pié Fourché, whose sale, initiated soon after the King's accession, had been a long drawn-out affair. On 3 March authority was granted to raise six thousand *livres* in this way; later the sum allowed was doubled and the City Council arranged a loan of 30,000 l.t. on the burghers of Paris. Negotiations with the King were not sweetened by the presence of Robert de Beauvais whose appointment as Contrôleur Général des Deniers Communs aroused dismay and wrath in the Councillors when they met on 17 January. The Privy Council ignored their feelings, though at a later date Henri II cancelled the appointment; predictably, the records reveal persistent rumblings of discontent against this official whom the Councillors eventually barred from their sessions and who was not allowed, in spite of royal support, to take his place in the municipal procession for the Entry.

Other matters caused friction. The question of allowances for the costumes and uniforms to be worn soon engaged the attention of the Council. Certain sums, proportionate to the status of the officials concerned, were authorised by the King—for instance the Councillors were to receive 50 l.t. each, the *quarteniers* 30 l.t., other grades the same amount as for previous Entries; but they were considered inadequate for the scale of ceremony envisaged. In the light of the royal authorization for increased expenditure under this item, the Council, which allowed satin and "doubleure" whereas hitherto no "doubleure" was permitted, raised the allowance for each grade (R, 160). So far as the Enfants de Paris were concerned, the Captain and Lieutenant (Germain Boursier and Drouet Parent respectively) were appointed in April; but the expense of providing their outfits was not met by public funds:

> L'habit estoit si riche et de si grand coust qu'il n'y auoit que les enffans des meilleures maisons de Paris qui voulsissent promectre à le fournir à leurs despens, et jusques au nombre qui sera descript à l'entrée dud. seigneur.   (R, 161)

Not surprisingly, pressure had to be brought to bear in May on the Enfants de Paris to make greater speed with their preparations (R, 162). Then, there were difficulties with the inhabitants of the houses situated on the Pont Notre-Dame: the most "honnestes personnages" of the town and the most distinguished "damoiselles" were to be present on the bridge, and to this end the "première chambre" of each house was to be set apart to accommodate the persons designated by the City Council. The householders, however, showed a marked reluctance to toe the line and the instructions of 7 April had to be renewed in the following months.

Plans were soon in train for the setting up of the decorations. On 3 March 1548 (n.s.1549), Charles le Conte, "maistre charpentier juré du roy," contracted with the City Council for a sum of 2000 l.t. to provide the woodwork and carpentry of the four triumphal arches, the "perspective devant le Chastelet" and the "piramide ou obelisque" (C, fol. 54 ff.); and further contracts were drawn up with Jehan Cousin, Charles Dorigny and Jehan Goujon for the "painctreries et figures" connected with these constructions "et autres lieux," to the tune of 3000 l.t. (ibid., fol. 56 ff.). On 16 March negotiations were completed with Jehan Cousin, goldsmith, Hance Yoncques, Thibault Laurens and Marc Begault for the fashioning of the City's present to the King, which was to cost 10,085 l. 6 s. 10 d.t. (ibid., fol. 113 ff.). Work went on apace, but proclamations had to be made threatening with hanging anyone who pilfered or damaged the arches and other decorations. On 6 March, the Archers had been given their orders for the Entry (R, 155); thought was also being given to the Queen's Entry and her present from the City; and towards the end of March contracts were passed for construction and decoration relating to the "festin, disner, recueil" due to take place in the Palace of the bishop of Paris, who at that time was in Rome (C, fol. 123v). For his part, the King was entertaining further plans for his Entry: on the one hand, he had decided to follow the ceremonies with a tourney, and on the other we learn on 14 May of plans for a naval combat on the Seine. Under the date of 3 May, on the initiative of M. de Lezigny, there had been an inspection of the sites with Charles le Conte and discussion of the arrangements for the *lices*; the unpaving of the rue Saint-Antoine was to be expedited, the *perron* at Saint-Lazare was to be built and Charles le Conte to undertake the carpentry work for the arches and other features (R, 162).[8]

The original intention that the Entry take place on 15 May had to be abandoned and a new date, 14 June, was fixed with due proclamation.[9] Needless to say, such postponement was to involve the City in further expense: payment for materials no longer suitable, additional pay and subsistence for some of those involved. However, once the King's plans were clear, he paid great attention to details of protocol and also to the features of the Entry that especially attracted him. He had been staying at Saint-Germain-en-Laye, but at Whitsuntide he came to Saint-

Denis, where he was welcomed by the Cardinal de Bourbon and touched the sick in the Abbaye cloisters. On Whitmonday (10 June), the *sacre*
and coronation of the Queen, Catherine de Médici, took place at Saint-
Denis; and the royal couple stayed there until the Entry into Paris. On
Tuesday of that same week the Entry of the Dauphin took place;[10] the
procession walked before him

> jusques à la porte Sainct Honnoré, où il y auoit plusieurs pieces
> d'artillerye qui feurent tirées à son entrée, et feirent grand bruyt.
> Et de là le menerent jusques au Palais, où il devait loger.

On 14 June the Dauphin received from the City his present of

> un bassin d'argent vermeil doré, cizelé d'antique, faict en façon
> d'oualle pesant unze marc quatre onces selon la pesée qui en a esté
> faicte en leur presence par Jehan Cousin marchant orfebure.
> (C, fol. 121)

It was handed over by the Prévôt des Marchands et Echevins "en une
gallerie près le Iardin du pallais," in the presence of the prince's gover-
nors:

> led. bassin estant remply de dragées dorées au meilleu desquelles
> estoit ung arbre de sucre doré auec douze grans bouettes espices à
> sa bienvenue et nouuelle arriuée en cestedicte ville.
> (C, fol. 121 r–v)

Throughout this same week there took place the "montre des
mestiers de Paris," though the procession from Saint-Antoine to the
bois de Vincennes was marred by heavy rain. Indeed, it was the exceptionally vile weather that introduced a last-minute hitch: on 13 June at
five o'clock in the afternoon, the King sent Maigny to the Hôtel de
Ville "pour les grandes inondations d'eaues, vent impetueux et incom-
modité du temps" (R, 163), and immediately orders were given
postponing the Entry until 16 June.[11] On the Saturday the command
was issued for everyone to be at his station next morning by 9 A.M.,
with the *gens de pied* on parade along the river at 4 A.M. (R, 164); the
mounted guards were to be ready by 10 A.M. at Saint-Martin des
Champs.

The days preceding the Entry had been troubled, not only by the
stormy weather, but by much squabbling and bickering over matters of

precedence. The University, which had been represented in Paris Entries since 1531, developed a row as to who should deliver the harangue
on its behalf; hitherto the duty had devolved upon a theologian, but at
a meeting called to discuss matters of precedence, Jean Marischal, professor of rhetoric at the Collège de Calvi, had proposed that the speech
be given by the Rector, on the grounds that other "compagnies" had
their head as spokesman. All faculties had concurred at the time; they
also decided, on a later occasion, to follow the advice of the Cardinal de
Lorraine who had suggested that the harangue be delivered, not according to previous custom in front of Sainte-Geneviève des Ardents, but
at Saint-Lazare, when and where other "compagnies" were to be received by the King; it was furthermore agreed that the University
representatives should proceed on horseback. The theologians,
however, preferred Shanks' mare, and indeed they made an issue of the
matter, chiefly because they felt aggrieved by these new arrangements.
They obtained a letter from the King forbidding the University "de ne
rien changer dans son ancien ceremonial"—a formula which they
maintained applied also to the question of who was to deliver the
harangue. Ultimately it was agreed to give way on the mode of
transport only and the Rector spoke on behalf of the University:

> Le Roi écouta le Recteur avec satisfaction, & lui fit une réponse
> pleine de bonté par l'organe du Chancelier Oliuier. Il voulut
> même que tous les suppôts de l'Université passassent comme en
> revue devant lui: distinction unique & qui ne fut accordée à
> aucune autre compagnie.[12]

Notwithstanding, the Deans of faculties felt they should stand next to
the Rector when he gave his speech, in order to report its substance
back to their members. This was agreed and came into effect for the
Queen's Entry, though the theologians, once again in the minority, expressed unhappiness at the change. In fact, on two further occasions, it
was a theologian who spoke for the University, but the new arrangements quickly found favor and became the established procedure.
    Trouble also arose among the *parlementaires,* as Du Tillet, Greffier du
Parlement de Paris, informs us:

> Ce iour (sc. 16 June) s'est assemblée la Cour au Palais enuiron
> neuf heures du matin, pour aller au deuant du Roy, lequel ce dit
> iour faisoit sa nouuelle Entrée en cette ville de Paris: & pour ce
> qu'il eut quelque differend entre les Huissiers de l'ancienne &

> nouuelle creation, fut ordonné que pour ces deux iours d'Entrée,
> sans preiudice des droicts des parties, ils marcheroient selon l'or-
> dre de leurs Receptions, & au premier iour ils seroient ouys &
> reglez sur leur differend. (God., I, 879)

It appears, too, that the "advocats & Procureurs du commun" were not
present to bring up the rear of the Parlement representatives on the day
(ibid., I, 880). In principle, the order of procession of the City officials
had been set down by the King in letters patent of 29 April (AN K 957,
pièce 15), but clearly not to the satisfaction of all concerned.

Closely allied to the question of precedence and representation was
that of costume. Renaissance France was very sensitive to the social
significance of dress, and throughout the century we come across
decrees (including some by Henri II) forbidding burghers and their
wives to wear apparel and finery above their station; fairly elaborate
rules, for instance, were drawn for the wearing of silk, and color was a
jealously guarded privilege. A few days before the King's Entry discord
broke out about the right of the members of the Cours des Aides and
the officials of the Châtelet to wear scarlet (see AN X^{IA} 1565 fol. 170v).
Moreover the lieutenant du bailli de Paris sought to enjoy the same
privilege, but the Court had no hesitation in blocking his claim "sous
peine de mil livres parisis d'amende" (God., I, 885). Louis Gayant,
conseiller au Parlement, presented the "defenses" given to the Cour des
Aides and the Châtelet to wear scarlet, and this was approved by the
Chancellor and finally the King himself. Nevertheless, the officials of
the Châtelet, on Saturday 15 June, were under the impression that
they at any rate were authorized by the King to don scarlet, mainly on
grounds of precedent for earlier Entries; but the Chancellor disclaimed
any knowledge of such royal permission and there was no change in the
official attitude. For his part, the Chancellor had expressed a possible
diplomatic wish to proceed with the representatives of the Parlement,
wearing scarlet, but — and this brings out one feature of the Entry — the
King

> vouloit fair son entrée en armée: & pour ce il entendoit que le dit
> Chancelier tinst ordre separé & portast robbe de drap d'or frizé, &
> qu'il falloit qu'il compleust à la volonté du Roy. (God., I, 886)

The Chancellor — in this instance François Olivier — was usually a
lawyer of distinction, but his position had become increasingly important during the sixteenth century, so that he had a say in matters

ranging far and wide, though the Connétable had oversight of military affairs.

B. The Entries of the King and the Queen

(III) The King's Entry (16 June)

The *Registres*, the historians of the University, Du Tillet and eyewitnesses help us to fill out the picture provided by the *livret*; there are some discrepancies on the times and orders of procession, though not to the point of serious conflict. The *livret* relates the order of procession as it follows the King entering his City, whereas the *Registres* list the participants as they assemble to meet the King. The procession went by

> son chemyn de la Greve droit à la rue Saint Denis et tout le long d'icelle jusques hors lad. Ville et tournerent sus les fossez jusques à Sainct Laurens, qui va aud. Sainct Lazare ès faulxbourgs Sainct Denis . . .   (R, 168)

Henri had been waiting to receive the various "compagnies" since 8 A.M. at Saint-Lazare (Saint-Ladre), seated on a chair covered in "veloux pers"; the chair was placed on "ung perron de boys deuant la rue Sainct Laurens" (R, 164), described more enthusiastically a few pages later as "un tribunal fort somptueux et magnifique." The procession, in view of the numbers,[13] took an unconscionable time to reach Saint-Lazare: the *Registres* talk of six hours, but Du Tillet contents himself with the laconic adverb "longuement." It was 11 A.M. by the time the last of the guilds had reached the royal stage. Since the *livret* records the order of procession, only other points need be noted here. The *Registres*, for instance, provide a much more detailed description of the costumes worn by the Enfants de Paris, whose splendor and indeed extravagance had been a matter of concern earlier; furthermore they had a Celtic flavor, intended to bring out the theme of France's distinction through the centuries. It seems also that there was trouble with the "libraires" who did not respect the arrangements and turned up in greater numbers than had originally been stipulated. In due course, the harangues were delivered on behalf of the several companies: Germain Boursier for the Enfants de Paris, Claude Guyot, Prévôt des Marchands, for the City (details in R, 168–69), the Premier Président for the Parlement (AN X^{IA}, 1965, fol. 172–174v) and the Rector for the University, with the Chancellor replying in the name of the King.

After receiving the various dignitaries, the King set out upon his Entry, with the different guilds bearing the "riche ciel de parement" over him along their appointed distances: the *échevins* from the Porte Saint-Denis to the Eglise de la Trinité; the drapers as far as "Sainct Leu Sainct Gilles"; the *épiciers* to Saint-Innocent; the *merciers* to Sainte-Opportune; the *pelletiers* on to the Châtelet; from there the *bonnetiers* carried the dais to Saint-Denis de la Chartre, and finally the *orfèvres* walked in procession to Notre-Dame. In the cortège, there were one or two unusual features: for instance, a riderless horse ("fleurdelysé") carried the mace and long sword: such a horse had figured previously in the royal funereal ceremony; and the royal sword was carried by the Connétable (acting also as Grand Master). Normally this duty was the prerogative of the master of the horse, who on such occasions carried the King's personal sword. The military significance of all this would not pass unnoticed.[14] In spite of the preliminary delays the *Registres* comment favorably on the women and crowds thronging the Pont Notre Dame: the women were "davantage tant bien parées que l'on eust plustost estimé au champ des bienheureux que sur un passaige terrestre, fondé sur l'eau d'une rivière" (R, 177). Contemporaries were also greatly impressed by the magnitude of the gunfire from 350 pieces of artillery that continued from morning until about four o'clock in the afternoon (R, 168); and everybody felt that this was "le plus magnifique triumphe qui iamais fut faict à Empereur ou Roy . . . et ne sçay s'il se pourra faire que la postérité le puisse egaller" (ibid.). All this splendor is reflected in the bill for the City: 40, 028 1. 9 s. 11 d.t. without taking into account the presents to the King, Queen and Dauphin or the disbursements made in connection with the tourney and the *naumachia* (C, fol. 142). On arriving at Notre-Dame the King was met by the clergy in front of the Cathedral; but this part of the ceremony had probably lost something of its former importance over the years.[15] After service the King, on horseback, went along the rue de la Calandre to the Palais de Justice.

In the evening, the royal banquet was held at the Palais, and here the *livret* is less explicit than Du Tillet who informs us that only princes

of the blood were seated at the royal table and that there was some
bickering among the princes on the order of seating, so that the matter
had to be settled by the King:

> (Il) iugea aussi le differend meu entre lesdicts Princes, voulans les
> uns seoir à la dextre selon la proximité de la Couronne, & declara
> qu'il donnoit sa dextre pour honnorer l'Eglise, & que les Princes
> de son Sang Laics doivent estre à la senestre en ladicte table. (Du
> Tillet, in God., I, 885; for further details of the supper, see R,
> 179)

Du Tillet also mentions, unlike the *livret,* the popular festivities that
took place that evening:

> Et tout ledit soir fut fait diuerses demonstrations de plaisirs &
> resiouyssances par les habitans de ladite Ville, qui s'estoient mis
> en toutes despences pour se parer, & recevoir honorablement ledit
> Seigneur en icelle.   (ibid.)

With the visit to the Palais de Justice, the King's Entry proper comes to
its appointed end, but there were related ceremonies and festivities to
follow.

(iv) The Queen's Entry (18 June)

Monday 17 June was a day of respite, for it was on the following day
that the King was received by the Estats de la Ville and that the Queen
made her Entry into the capital. The municipal procession set out as
early as 8 A.M. to welcome her (R, 179); and Du Tillet states that the
representatives of the Parlement foregathered at about 10 A.M. and that
the Queen made her Entry at about 3 P.M. (God., I, 887). Her *sacre*
had taken place on 10 June and an account was issued to com-
memorate the occasion: published by J. Dallier, it serves apparently as
a pendant to the *livret* of the King's Entry. Traditionally, the Queen's
Entry had been associated with the theme of peace and, therefore, prosperity. One interesting fact has emerged about the preparations: it
was Philibert de l'Orme, on the instructions of Montmorency, who was
commissioned to erect the stand in Notre-Dame.[16] He called on the
services of Jehan Allemand, "maistre des oeuvres de charpenterie du
roy"; this craftsman was also employed at the Arsenal in July 1549, at

the Sainte-Chapelle du Bois de Vincennes in June 1550 and later in the same year at the Château de Boulogne. In Notre-Dame a large stand was erected in front of the high altar, four others in the choir for the princes, the knights of the order of Saint Michael, the ambassadors and the ladies of the Queen's household, and in the lower wings of the choir two further stands to accommodate the noblemen and the ladies of the Court. To the right of the altar was a small construction from which the King could watch the proceedings without himself being seen; and to the left was a stand for the choir. This is not the only occasion on which we shall glimpse Philibert de l'Orme's hand in the Entry. The official records devote much space to matters of precedence and to the personalities involved; the costumes worn were in many instances different from those donned for the King's Entry. Thus we learn that

> les Enffans des bonnes maisons de lad. ville (were) au mesme ordre qu'ilz furent à l'entrée du Roy, excepté que à lad. entrée du Roy ilz avoient chemises de maille, ilz portoient aucuns d'eulx pourpointz de satin blanc chiqueté. (R, 179)

In the evening the Royal supper took place at the Palais, and on this the *livret* gives us a number of details. Belleforest offers a touch of color in his description, short as it is, of the Queen's Entry:

> Mais sur tout la Royne & madame Marguerite de France, assises de front en une litiere descouuerte, & suiuies des Princesses, Duchesses, Comtesses, & Dames de France: mesmes de trois chariots triomphans, plus enrichis de beautez & graces des Damoyselles qu'ils portoyent, que de la crouste & drap d'argent qui les couuroient iusques en terre, distrayoient les regardans en triple admiration par leurs dignitez, beautez & tresprecieux accoustremens.[17]

On the morrow the Queen attended Mass in Notre-Dame, together with the King who had to accede to the Dean's request that the numerous gate-crashers settled in the cloisters during the King's Entry be evicted (AN LL 248, fol. 710, 712). That evening the City offered a banquet to the Queen, not, as it had been hoped in the Hôtel de Ville, because it was "incommode pour le bastiment neuf que l'on faict d'iceluy" (C, fol. 125), but instead in the palace of the Bishop of Paris, Jean du Bellay. Special decorations were undertaken in connection with the banquet, though it appears that the painting of Peleus and

Thetis (mentioned in the *livret*) was already in the episcopal residence.
The *Comptes* offer a more elaborate description of these decorations
which were carried out by Jehan Cousin, Charles Dorigny and Jehan
Goujon; they were paid 750 l.t. for having

> faict & parfaict les ouuraiges de paintrerie qu'ilz avoient promis
> faire tant en ladicte grant salle que dehors pour la decorer pour le
> iour dud. festin, comme il s'ensuict. C'est assauoir fait le plancher
> et les costez d'icelle salle de toille et cordes garnies. Lesdictes cor-
> des . . . couuertes de liarre et bouys et autres choses dorees et le
> fons dud. plancher faict par parquetz de compartments ou
> estoient appliquees /hh/ et chiffres croissans et auec turquois rosés
> et grotesques, doré, azuré et painct de belles et unies coulleurs.
> Item faict aux deux costez et deux boutz de lad. salle par hault au
> dessus dud. plancher une frize de compartmens de neuf piez de
> hault où estoient applicquez grans carrez de paincture faictz en
> paisages dhistoires poeticques et alentour grosses bordures de
> painctures et de bouys vert tortillé d'or au costé dud. carré fait des
> grotesques de coulleurs en champ blanc et entre lesd. grotesques
> estoient des niches dans lesquelles estoient figures de dieux et
> deesses de coulleur de marbre blanc. Au dessoubz desd. niches
> tables d'actente dedans lesquelles y auoit quelque mot ou grotes-
> que applicqué. Au dessus des granz carrez les armoiries du roy,
> aux ungs et aux autres les armoiries de la royne. Au meilleu de la
> bordure d'un grant carré une masque à l'antique et aux deux
> costez grotesques tant hault que bas et le corps et fons tout de
> pierre mixte et iaspe. Item faict huict chassis de cinq piez et demy
> de hault et deux piez de large de fine toille blanche painctz de
> grotesques de coulleur et croix de cyre blanche de Venise qui ont
> esté mis en lad. grant salle aux fenestres et croisées d'icelle. Item
> faict ung berceau de lyarre depuis la porte de l'eglise nostre dame
> de paris jusques dedans lad. grant salle garny d'armoiries du roy
> et de la royne auec autres deuises et compartment; le tout faict de
> bonnes et unies painctures . . .   (C, fol. 125–26)

The contract was negotiated on 30 March, and payment made on 30
June. Charles le Conte was responsible for building a wooden bridge
and staircase from Notre-Dame to the episcopal palace for the benefit
of the Queen, and he had to arrange for the erection of a small platform
on which the musicians hired for the banquet were to perform (C, fol.
101 ff. and 107v). The presentation of the gift and the speech were

made by Claude Guyot. The augmented *livret,* after noting that the dancing preceded the banquet, has something to say about the present given to the Queen, but the most detailed description is to be found in the *Comptes* (fol. 118v-19):

> A Pierre Hotman, marchant bourgeois de Paris La somme de sept mil neuf cens trois livres deux solz six deniers tournois . . . pour auoir . . . fourny et liuré le buffet de vaisselle d'argent vermeil doré, cyzelée de croissans et de fleurs de liz cy après déclaré, C'estassauoir une navire du poix de cinquante huict marcs six onces, ung pot de trente huict marcs six onces pesant, ung autre pot du poix de trente deux marcs demye once, une buye pesant trente trois marcs trois onces, deux flacons du poix de vingt trois marcs quatre onces, deux vases du poix de unze marcs six onces
> ` (*between the lines:* deux grans bassins pesant vingt trois marcs six onces). Trois sallieres dont une couuerte du poix de six marcs trois onces six gros, six grans tasses et deux couuercles pesans cinquante sept marcs six onces et demye. Quatre chandelliers à flambeaulx pesans vingt deux marcs cinq onces et demye et quatre couppes couuertes du poix de quinze marcs et une once six gros . . .

After dinner, the King and the Queen attended vespers in Notre-Dame.

On 20 June it was the King's turn to receive his present from the City and we have already seen the sum which the City was prepared to spend on its fabrication. The details of this elaborate piece of craftsmanship, though omitted in certain issues of the *livret,* are given in the augmented version.[18] Not only does the workmanship appear to have been exquisite, but it was a study in royal symbolism: the continuity of the monarchy was expressed in the presentation of three successive kings, each associated with some royal attribute—wisdom, justice and, in Henri II's case, military prowess, which emphasizes a major theme of the whole Entry. After receiving his present, the King, in accordance with precedent, accepted the invitation to go to the Grève on the following Sunday, 23 June (the feast of St. John the Baptist) in order to light the bonfire or "arbre" in honor of the saint.

Before we pass to the tourney and the *naumachia,* it will be convenient to look at the principles that underlie the Royal Entry. It is simplest, first to note the leitmotive; then we should look at the Royal route, mentioning more especially the architectural features; and before analyzing in detail literary and artistic elements of the Entry, we shall examine briefly the political aspects which underlie the ceremonies and often appear in the detail of the various constructions.

(v) Major Themes of the Entry

In the preparations for the Entry there converge a number of currents, some of which are predictable in the nature of things. Obviously, the Entry affords the capital city a chance to affirm its status, and we have seen that delays and the efforts of Lyon in the previous year did nothing to diminish that urge. In a broader political context, it serves to assert France's prominence, indeed dominance on the European stage, and the challenge to the Emperor Charles V is never far below the surface. Nearer at home, the Entry stresses the authority of the King in a country where the situation, especially on the religious front, is not all that stable. In addition, the pageantry will suggest ambivalence to the past: on the one hand, one notes the desire to prolong the more impressive traditions of France and on the other, an equally strong desire to improve on the achievements of the previous reign. For instance, the exploitation of the *Hercule gaulois* theme could be conveniently harmonized with the myth of the Trojan origins of French monarchy; and this would not only suggest a glorious past, but also give France a cultural and historical precedence over Rome. We are in a period, moreover, when the Renaissance emphasis on parade and *paraître,* accompanied by Henri II's taste for greater formality and splendor, takes on noteworthy proportions. As the *livret* and other sources make abundantly clear, the sense of national distinction is to find expression in a new aesthetic underlying the architectural and artistic features of the Entry. In this same year, there appears the *Deffense et illustration de la langue françoyse,* written by Joachim du Bellay and offering a blueprint for the renewal of French literature. The Pléiade was not involved in the preparations for the Entry; but neo-classical ideals are making themselves felt in the artistic circles of the Court, a phenomenon that is associated with the favor shown by Henri II to artists less prominent under his father, though once again we cannot speak of a total break with the past. Finally, the Entry is, it seems, unusual compared with previous pageants on account of the immense trouble and care taken to plan and coordinate the various aspects of the ceremonies and the artistic features: this shows itself also in the

systematic development of major themes (themselves not necessarily
new) in the Entry and particularly in the progression of architectural
structures along the Royal route. This will be reflected, not only in the
neo-classical principles of art, but also in the complex use made of
mythological and other symbolism.

The first theme is that of Force and Authority, a traditional theme,
of course, but strikingly developed by recourse to the classical myth of
Hercules. The presence of Hercules in French Royal Entries is nothing
new, for it goes back as far as 1486, but here it is more amply
developed. The *livret* points out explicitly that the face of the hero on
the first triumphal arch "se rapportoit singulièrement bien à celuy du
feu Roy François"; nor is this the only occasion on which Henri's
ancestors are brought into the picture. Andrea Fulvio draws attention
to the links between Hercules and classical triumphs:

> Fu da Euandro consagrata nel Foro Boario la statua d'Hercole,
> che era chiamata trionfale, & per ciò vestita in habito trionfale. Fu
> anchora da Numa Re consagrata la statua di Iano Gemino, cioè
> di due faccie.[19]

But Hercules had acquired a special appeal for French humanists;
recent research has stressed the contemporary relevance of a deity
whose legends had conferred upon him a Greek, a Libyan, a Gallic and
a Germanic countenance — to which was also to be added a Christian
dimension.[20] The legend of the Gallic Hercules, which emphasized the
civilizatory role of the god as well as fitting into French humanist myths
about national origins, was a most suitable symbol; but the aspect of
Hercules the soldier and conqueror (i.e. the Libyan) is far from dis-
counted here — indeed one may feel that the Libyan Hercules has been
overassimilated to the Gallic, in that Gaulish military prowess is made
much of in the entry. Hercules' significance is brought out in Germain
Boursier's harangue which, though omitted from the *livret,* is recorded
in the *Registres* (169):

> Deux Hercules ont esté, l'ung de Libye, qui par force plusieurs
> monstres combatit, et de vaillance le lotz emporta; l'autre des
> Gaulles, qui de belle eloquence, prudence et iustice fut, qui
> premier les Celtes, par les champs espanduz, ès villes et ensemble
> vivre et batailler enseigna. Mais ces deux pour ung tiers parfaict
> en vous se sont assemblez, et ce que Libye et Gaulles ont eu et
> n'ont point eu, la France en vous a recouuert, qui sans la massue,

les vices vrays abattez et les rebelles à obeyssance ramenez, et de vostre seul nom les villes closes faictes deuant vous saillir à plain les tirez.

The closing lines allude to Henri II's military activities since his accession — and 1548 had also seen the fierce repression of sedition in Bordeaux at the hands of Anne de Montmorency; the reference to Hercules' destruction of monsters will also be found in the *livret,* where it is explained that he carried a lance with a serpent entwined about it, which signified "prudence en guerre." The Hercules myth was also associated with Charles V: Claude Paradin reminds us that the *devise* of the two columns "que l'antiquité a nommé les deux colonnes d'Hercules," had been adopted by the German Emperor — and, more cogently, the Hercules theme had figured in his Entry into Paris nearly ten years previously;[21] to politically sensitive contemporaries such nuances would not pass unnoticed. In the *livret,* so far as the first triumphal arch is concerned, it is the cultural aspects of Hercules that are prominent: he is represented as leading the four estates by persuasion rather than by force, though cynical contemporaries probably took a different view.[22] John Stewart — a Scottish humanist who became the Principal of a Paris college — makes the following comments in an *Oratio* on the Royal Entry:

Asia priscis temporibus Liberum patrem victorem gentium & populorum, & Herculem Liberi patris aemulum, itemque Alexandrum magnum, qui utriusque vestigia passibus aequis emensus est, non humanis, sed diuinis honoribus & gratulationibus est prosequutus . . . [23]

Incidentally, the legend stressed that Hercules, a human, was raised to divine status after his death, a detail that would not be out of place in pageantry of this sort.

The labors of Hercules are not given much space, but educated contemporaries would, partly in the wake of Alciat, associate them with virtue and self-control. On the other hand, the Entry organizers made a slightly clumsy allusion to the Hercules who appears in the legend of the Argonauts, no doubt to provide a handy transition to the theme of the Argosy and the Golden Fleece. Though the military aspects of the God are far from played down, his other attributes — prudence, eloquence, civilization, virtue, self-discipline — are duly represented; but the *Registres* (171) make special reference to the victorious nature of the monarch:

> Tout homme de bon iugement peult congnoistre que les deux der-
> niers vers sont à la louenge du Roy Henry triumphateur, de qui
> l'esperance est plus grande que l'on ne la sauroit escripre.

This theme of triumph appears early in the sections relating to motifs
based on the Argosy and to the arch "où se pouuoit veoir debout un
Typhis de dix pieds en stature, dont la figure approchoit bien fort de
celle du Roy triumphateur" (*livret,* fol. 13v). That contemporaries
grasped the parallel between the Argonauts and Henri with his nobles
emerges clearly from a remark in John Stewart's oration, which con-
cludes the list of the Argonauts figuring in the Entry as follows:

> id est, nobiles Galliae principes, qui Henrico regi vastum & im-
> mensum imperij pelagus intranti dicerunt.[24]

The royal colors, black and silver, were woven into the fabric of the
arch and into the description of Castor and Pollux, who carried stars
symbolizing immortality or renewal of life. The military prowess of
France is given further emphasis apropos of the Seine wearing a laurel
wreath:

> . . . & certes à tort, au moings si l'on veult iuger sans affecta-
> cion, consideré que ses enffans ont esté, sont & peuuent estre
> aussi bien triumphateurs que les Romains et autres peuples
> precedens, et n'a tenu sinon à ceulx qui debvoient escripre, les-
> quelz vivoyent du temps de nos ancestres, que leurs gestes dignes
> de l'immortalité ne soyent parvenuz jusques à nous; et si cela feust
> succédé par avanture, n'aurions nous occasion d'admirer les faicts
> des estrangiers, ains verrions que si nos Gaulois ne les surpassent,
> ilz pour le moings les peuvent egaller. Mais soit icy modestie
> gardée, pour revenir à nostre fleuve . . .   (R, 173)

Care was also taken to point out the two Victories on the triumphal
arch; the present to the King showed his association with Mars, a symbol of "noblesse françoyse," and two Gaulish commanders were selected
to adorn the H-shaped arch, with the significant mottoes: *Mars
Gallorum Deus* and *Dis Gallorum pater.* So far as the symbolism of the
Argosy is concerned, spectators would probably remember two
features in particular: the order of the Golden Fleece had been founded
in 1430 by Philip of Burgundy and, as Paolo Giovio reminds us, was

the object of Charles V's marked attention. Henri could be seen as try-
ing to take over the symbolism of the Golden Fleece to his advantage.
The other feature was of course the Argo itself: broadly it would be
linked with the ship of state, successfully piloted, but the ship was also
the emblem of the City of Paris. Claude Paradin's fanciful account is
none the less valuable for its contemporary reference. In connection
with the motto *En altera quae vehat Argo* he writes:

> Les Franques ou François (peuple iadis frequentant la marine, &
> gens exerçans l'Art Piratique, selon Latinus Pacatus, Sidon
> Apollinaris & Beatus Rhenanus) voulurent que le lieu principal
> auquel ils s'estoyent arrestez, qui est la cité de Paris, capitale de
> France, portast perpetuellement l'enseigne de la profession & art
> dont ils se mesloyent. Parquoy lui donnerent la Deuise de Nauire,
> qu'elle a depuis tousiours porté iusques à present. Et n'est pas in-
> conuenient, que iceux ne participassent des Gepides, lesquelz
> aussi au parauant se remerquoyent du Nauire, frequentans la
> mer Germanique, nation possible Troyenne, & escartée en loin-
> taines mers, apres la destruction de Troye, de laquelle l'opinion
> commune tient, que les nobles de France sont descendus.[25]

The importance of this motif is that it is developed in terms of both
King and City. The City would no doubt appreciate the Argonauts'
wish to follow the King on the journey to success. The symbolism at
this point is somewhat complex, and if we take up a suggestion by
Bryant,[26] it may well be that though a certain aggressivity is evident,
the motto — in fact a tag from Vergil's IVth eclogue, opens up other
possibilities. That eclogue, with its messianic associations, suggests the
advent of a new era: the new Typhis and heroic age that anticipate the
coming of Saturn and the return of Justice (Astraea). If these covert
Vergilian echoes are accepted, then Henri II (seen shortly as *Genius
princeps*) would be the harbinger of a new era of peace and prosperity.

The theme of Abundance pervades the text and, as is noted by
sixteenth-century authorities, its major symbol is the cornucopia which
has the advantage of association with many mythological figures, some
of whom make their appearance in the Entry. *Abondance* is mentioned
early in reference to *Gallia fertilis* (*livret*, fol. 6v), a formula that
presumably goes back to Livy (V. 34. 2) and is inscribed on the arch in
front of Saint-Jacques de l'Hôpital, where various features are made to
converge on the figure of Gallia. She bears many flowers and fruits "de
sa production"; beneath the inscriptions are two children leaning on

cornucopiae; the elegiac couplet, the first line of which is taken from the *Aeneid* I. 531, stresses three characteristics of France: her antiquity, her soldierly distinction, and her fertility. This last trait is underscored yet again in the inscriptions mentioned on fol. 7v of the *livret: Matri piae* (associated with the capital city, but also with Mother Earth); and *Populorum omnium alumnae,* a phrase reminiscent of Pliny, III. 5. 6 *39 *Itala omnium terrarum alumna eadem et parens* (*alumna* meaning "nourisher"). The theme of abundance is then transferred to the two rivers Seine and Marne represented on this arch; the urn of the Seine (*ubertas*) is graced with fruit, "par especial de bledz & de raisins," and the Marne, whose Latin name *Matrona* is ambiguous, serves as a companion figure. The organizers may well have been influenced by the two-river motif exploited in the Lyon Entry; but there is in any case a tendency in the Paris ceremonies towards binary themes and figures, encouraged no doubt by the architectural symmetry. *Bonus Eventus* is flanked by Flora and Pomona whose symbolism needs no stressing, apart from "un vray lys naturel," which presumably refers to the flower of France, but might also be a discreet hommage to Catherine de Médici in that the lily had Florentine associations. In the French quatrains (*livret,* fol. 8v), the theme is further enriched by the Cybele motif, a goddess traditionally associated with the Earth, but whom the poets of the Pléiade link with Catherine herself. *Bonus Eventus* takes his place opposite Gallia ("seoit un bon Evenement vestu d'un habit simple, tenant en sa main droicte une coupe d'or, & en l'autre une poignée d'espiz de blé suyuant la description des antiques"). The main classical portrait of this deity occurs in Pliny (XXXIV. 8. 19 *77), who adds poppies to the *espiz.* Described by Lewis and Short as a "guardian deity of the Roman husbandmen," here he brings together more closely the themes of Abundance and Fortune; and as Cartari points out, the statue of *Bonus Eventus* was placed next to that of Fortune in the Capitol.[27]

This tendency to multiply the symbolic reference of features and figures of the Entry appears in the use made of the cornucopia acting as a link device. According to Cartari, it was associated with the legend of Hercules after his passion for Amalthea, but elsewhere with Fortune. The motif of Hercules and the origin of the cornucopia is mentioned by Du Bellay in his poem for the Entry and elucidated by "J. P."[28] In the Entry it appears apropos of the first figure of Fortune as well as with *Bonus Eventus*; and it is reinforced by another symbol of abundance, this time cultural abundance, in the portrayal of Minerva beneath the double triumphal arch facing the Palais de Justice (*livret,* fol. 27v). The fruit symbolism has been well exploited elsewhere in the Entry, but the mammary motif in this context is more unusual. According to Tervarent, commenting on *Femme qui presse le sein,* it is normally connected with Clemency, Venus and lasciviousness, but not learning.[29] The motif had appeared in the Rheims Entry at the time of the *sacre,* with "une fille richement parée" representing "Charité Reyne des vertus." If, as is possible, the Entry planners gave their own twist to a traditional symbol, we have an example of independence, but also of a desire to organize symbolism on an impressive scale. Of course, the normal attributes of Minerva are given expression here: learning, wisdom and prudence (a theme also developed under the aegis of Hercules). One may speculate on the motives underlying her presence here. Marguerite de France, the patroness-to-be of the Pléiade was associated by contemporaries with Minerva; but thanks to the transfer of certain attributes of Ceres, she is made to fit the pattern more closely. There may be another explanation: the statue was intended to enhance the prestige of Justice and the Parlement. The *livret* comments that, had Minerva been before Paris on Mount Ida, his famous judgment would have gone in her favor—so that she is seen to combine wisdom, power and beauty.[30]

The third major theme, on which we have inevitably touched already, is Fortune. It appears chiefly, as one would expect, on the Fontaine du Ponceau (or de la Reine), rebuilt in the time of Francis I. There was an obvious "social" symbolism with Jupiter at the apex, denoting Divine authority, and the three Fortunes (gold, silver, lead) representing justice, the nobles and the *tiers état.* In the first place, we have the use of a further ambivalent symbol, the rudder (fol. 4v) mentioned in reference to the King and connected in ancient times with both Fortune and abundance. Cartari observes that Lactantius graces Fortune with the attributes of both the cornucopia and the rudder, "comme etant en elle de donner les richesses, & de gouverner les affaires humaines, & les biens temporels."[31] Some also believed that Fortune accompanied "eloquence" and "doctrine," a theme developed by Jehan Cousin the younger in his *Livre de Fortune.*[32] In the second place, as Tervarent remarks, there emerges a Renaissance tradition, perhaps initiated but certainly fostered by Alciat, whereby Fortune and Virtue are no longer contraries, but in a sense collaborators.[33] Claude Paradin includes in his collection of *devises* one called *Virtutis Fortuna Comes* and tells us that it belonged to Timotheus, duke of Athens.[34] The various inscriptions *Regnorum sors diva comes* and *Sors fida potentum* develop the cognate theme, on which Giraldi has something to say, namely that kingship and fortune go hand in hand. The point is also made by John Stewart:

Quid secunda fortuna ad res magnas bene gerendas optabilius.[35]

Here we have a good example of the various ways in which humanist currents have filtered into the Entry. On the other themes exploited and centering explicitly on the King, Paris and France, little need be said here: certain attributes of the monarchy are mentioned or taken for granted (reason, virtue and especially prudence); what is emphasized is the superiority of France in so many domains, its abundance, divided by only a thin line from aggressiveness, and the support given to the country by supernatural powers embodied in Fortuna or Sors, behind which lie no doubt the expected Christian assumptions. Particularly impressive is the manner in which these motifs are orchestrated and interwoven by the use of multivalent classical symbols. At the same time it is important to see to what extent the Gaulish origins of the country are emphasized: this reflects certain trends in humanist research,[36] but it also expresses a pronounced nationalism. France's past is not rejected, indeed it is enhanced. Though such ideas appear more prominently at certain stations, it is an abiding concern of the Entry. They fit in with the myth of the *Hercule gaulois*; they mirror the legend of the Trojan kings, allegedly the ancestors of the French monarchy — a fanciful theory invented it seems by Berosius but useful in contexts where French cultural superiority might be claimed over the Greeks, Romans or indeed Germans. So far as Gaul is concerned, the Entry makes a good deal of its military supremacy — which masks certain cultural deficiencies: Brennus and Belgius who scored victories over Rome are given some prominence; the point is made apropos of the *Gallia fertilis* station — "La Gaule est mere commune à tous les peuples" and the theme is further brought out in the *Registres* (173) — and the Enfants de Paris were splendidly attired to look like Gaulish warriors.

(VI) Architectural Matters

What is especially striking about the Entry is the architectural
dimension, not merely its Roman, neo-classical character, but the
thoroughness and order with which this was taken into account. Contemporaries were forcibly impressed thereby, and John Stewart makes
much of it in his oration:

> Ornatus vix fuit eiusmodi, ut cum eum cupide & studiose spec-
> tarem, antiquam speciem & imaginem triumphi Romani videre
> mihi viderer, qualem in historiis descriptam & expressam
> legimus. Ut enim extra urbem in Vaticano, sic extra ad
> Coenobium Diui Lazari territorium triumphale fuit: & ut illic
> porta Capena triumphalis erat, qua currus imperatoris in-
> grederetur.[37]

Among the organizers are men imbued with neo-classical ideals: Jean
Martin, Jehan Goujon, Philibert de l'Orme, Jehan Cousin, to mention
the more conspicuous. In these circumstances, the *livret* may
understandably give the impression of a guidebook on architecture, a
point taken up in a derogatory way by the *livret* of the Rouen Entry in
1550.[38] In a sense, the *livret* is an *ouvrage de vulgarisation*, but it sheds
much light on the whole enterprise in the matter of the aesthetic principles involved.[39] Much care is taken to state the precise length and
height of various features (the columns in particular), and if there is a
departure from fundamental principle, a comment may be inserted, as
for instance on the arch at the nearer end of the Pont Notre-Dame:

> . . . la face du dedens oeuvre, combien qu'elle ne feust la prin-
> cipalle, mais à raison qu'elle se presentoit en veue la premiere.
>   (R, 177)

We have clear proof that Jean Martin was the chief planner. Secretary
to the seigneur de Lenancourt, he had carved out for himself a name as
a translator, an activity which we shall see affects his views on the
French language: among the books he had translated or was in the process of translating were *Horus Apollo* (1543), *Le Songe de Poliphile* (1546),
Serlio's treatise on architecture of which he had translated three books
by 1547, the Vitruvius published in the same year. He was already
engaged on his rendering of Leo Battista Alberti which was to appear
posthumously in 1553. Henri II, while he was still Dauphin, had taken

an interest in Martin and instructed him to translate Bembo's *Asolani* (1545), and the Vitruvius is dedicated to the new King. Jehan Goujon, originally architect to Anne de Montmorency, had soon entered the service of the King; he had collaborated in the publication of the Vitruvius and was involved in the erection of the Fontaine des Innocents which, in the view of his most recent biographer, may well owe something to Serlio's fourth Book.[40] We are still rather meagerly informed about Jehan Cousin — the identities of father and son are sometimes blurred — but a perusal of his *Livre de perspective*, printed shortly before his death in 1560, shows the sympathy he had with neo-classical principles and gives us an idea of his participation in 1549.[41] Philibert de l'Orme's role in the Entry is known up to a point, but he too fits into the neo-classical pattern. He had very clear ideas on the status and duties of the architect and seems to have done much to raise the standing of his profession, whereas before the builder was not easily distinguished from the master mason and was more subject to the whims of his masters. Above all, he stressed the need for the architect to be technically proficient and well educated, though he did not sin by excess and give equal weight to all the liberal arts.[42] No doubt, all these men and the more recent theoreticians they studied profess their admiration for Vitruvius who favors various principles put into practice in the 1549 Entry; but the adherence is not slavish, for on the one hand, all agreed that Vitruvius was often extremely obscure and sometimes incomplete, and on the other, a man such as Philibert de l'Orme insisted strongly on the right of a modern architect to indulge his fancy and use his powers of invention.

There is however some attempt to exploit the five orders systematically, so that not only are the proportions of each order fairly respected, but the symbolism attached to the order is also taken into account. A useful summary is furnished by Guillaume du Choul in a work published a few years later:

> Et de cecy nous rendra certains Vitruve au septiesme chapitre du premier livre, qui a mis le triumphe de Mercure dedans le marché, d'Apollo & de Libre Pater, auprès du theatre; à Hercules dedans les citez . . . En son troisiéme & quatriéme liure de l'Architecture il a mis la façon & maniere des temples, qui doibuent estre edifiez aux Dieux & Deesses, & par quel moyen ils doibuent estre architectez. C'est assauoir à Minerue, Mars & Hercules Doriques, pour ce qu'ils demandent, & si est requis, que les temples pour leurs vertus soyent sans delices. A Venus,

> Flora & Proserpine, & aux Nimphes des fontaines d'ordre Corin-
> the, pour ce qu'à ces Deesses pour leur delicatesse, les colonnes
> doibuent estre plus gresles, enrichies de fueillages, & de volutes,
> pour augmenter leur iuste & raisonnable decoration . . . [43]

and he goes on to observe that Juno and Diana are linked with the
Ionic order. Du Choul, incidentally, was with Maurice Scève and
Claude de Taillemont responsible for planning the Lyons Entry of
1548.

In his preface to Jean Martin's translation of Vitruvius, Jehan Goujon had claimed that, of the various sciences required in architecture,
geometry and perspective stood out; and he showed how important a
role was played by Serlio in acclimatizing Vitruvian principles in
France, an achievement to which had also contributed the seigneur de
Clagny (i.e. Pierre L'Escot) and "nostre maistre Philibert de l'Orme."[44]
It may well be that Serlio's treatise was instrumental in shaping the
aesthetic underlying the Entry, in these respects at any rate; but clearly
we are in the presence of a team informed by the same principles and
working together harmoniously. The *livret* reflects this concern with
geometry and one of the striking features of the whole ceremony was
the *Perspective* in which Lutetia appeared as Pandora.

There is a further, important aspect of this aesthetic and here surely
Alberti is the major influence. The *livret* refers to "Leur renflement pris
sur la tierce partie & demie de toute la tige mesurée en sept diuisions
egales" (fol. 6v), but the *Registres* (172) add "selon la reigle qu'en baille
messire Leon Baptiste Albert, qui faict monstrer l'ouurage de trop
meilleure grace que celle de Vitruve." Here we are dealing with a
technical point, but the word "grace" gives a clue. Alberti, who as much
as Philibert de l'Orme and others, underlines the standing of the architect, not only asserts the importance of symmetry, harmony and
perspective, but is convinced that a piece of architecture should appear
"natural" to the eye and also be graceful and pleasing to the beholder.
The *Registres* mention the "realistic" character of the Fontaine du
Ponceau (172) and the *livret* is studded with comments of this nature.
The Corinthian capitals, with their acanthus motif, were so remarkable
that "il sembloyt à la veue esblouyssante par trop les contempler
qu'elles undoyassent au vent" (fol. 6v); later, other capitals have "la
disposition du fueillage emulateur de la nature" (fol. 12v). Certain
figures at the far end of the Pont Notre-Dame were "tant bien exprimez
au naturel, que l'on ne se pouoit assouuir de les regarder" (fol. 16v).
The *Registres* (170), after noting the "linge de drapperye" of the *termini*

on the first triumphal arch, add "Quant est de leurs cheueulx & barbes, cela estoit si bien mené et renfondu par vraye intelligence que sembloit proprement que le vent les feist mouuoir." It is on grounds of realism that so much importance is attached to perspective, but other criteria, such as "grace" and the ubiquitous "doulceur" have their place too.

Thus we have an aesthetic based on reason, harmony, realism, perspective, but also delectation, and implemented by a team of men of ability and conviction. They owe much to Vitruvius and his more recent exponents; they may also be indebted to the *Songe de Poliphile*; one can hardly claim that this rather eccentric work has inspired the ensemble of any of the arches, but certain details may have stuck in the minds of the organizers, even if sometimes the features are themselves derivative: the stress on the obelisk (represented in a full-page plate of the *Songe*), the different types of column, the elephant underpinning the obelisk, the hieroglyphic element, the harpies as supporting figures, the poetry of ruins, the emphasis on fountains — though the route itself imposed such features — perhaps even the topiarism of the *Isle Cythere*. Nevertheless, the influence of the neo-classical treatises on architecture is more fundamental; and it is essentially through this tradition that the Entry assumes some of the features associated with Roman triumphs. John Stewart was quick to notice this, as we have already seen.

It is now time to look at the various features adorning the Royal route, though the next section will concern itself primarily with the artistic and architectural elements rather than with the symbolism which requires separate treatment.

(VII) The Royal Route

(a) The Porte Saint-Denis (*livret* fol. 1)

The outer portal was "d'ouurage Tuscan & Dorique"; the Doric element harmonizes with the Hercules theme, as Du Choul's remark indicates. The Tuscan order, closely related, is of the correct height or thereabouts, and is characterized by the presence of the arcade: Serlio brings out the links between the two orders, stressing the essentially rustic nature of the Tuscan — though in Roman times the rustic elements could be associated with orders other than the Doric. The arch is Doric, as are the bases on which the *termini* (styled *colosses* in the *livret* and *vates* by John Stewart) are standing; one suspects that Serlio is the inspiration here. On the one hand, the term "proportion diagonée" reflects the Italian's "proportione diagonea," and on the other the linking of Tuscan and Doric with the theme of Force is reminiscent of Serlio's observation: "la qual mistura, per mio aviso, e molto grata à l'occhio, e rappresenta in se gran fortezza."[45]   Elsewhere Serlio describes a rustic door which he believes would be very fitting "al palazzo di un soldato";[46] the Doric order was of course sacred to Jupiter and Mars as well as to Hercules. Serlio notes, with the help of a suitable illustration, the use of more rough-hewn stone for the arch itself ("cioè pezzi di pietre abbozzate cosi grossamente");[47] he introduces cracks into the walls and flowers growing out of them in his own illustrations. He also comments on the type of ornament used in the "berceau" which in principle is close to that used in the Entry:

> Alcuni altri Architetti hanno voluto usar maggior delicatezza, e piu ordinato compartimento, nondimeno tutta tal'opera ha hauuto origine de l'opera Rustica, ancora che communemente si dice a punte di diamante.[48]

Thus the rustic elements of the Entry are justified by the architectural authorities. The *Registres* at this point (and elsewhere) go in for more technical detail than the *livret*, notably in the matter of the capitals. The powerful muscular realism of the statue of Hercules (as well as Typhis) has encouraged some critics to think of Michaelangelo, and there may well be some influence here;[49] P. du Colombier sees a link between the Italian and Jehan Goujon.[50] The *Registres* (171) add a little about the musicians who played to the King:

> Puis se trouvant en ung pourpris quarré hipethrique ou à descouvert, entre les deux portes de la ville, dont les costez estoient tenduz de riche tappisserye, les musiciens à ce depputez lui feirent oyr une trop plus doulce armonye que n'avoit esté le bruyt des canons ordonnez sur les rampars . . .

(b) The Fontaine du Ponceau (or de la Royne) (fol. 4v)

The pilaster is described in the *livret* as Ionic, though no reference is made to the panels on which can be seen Nymphs and monsters. From another angle, the *Registres* (172) show how the criteria of realism work against an earlier tradition:

> Le Roy donc, ayant passé ceste fontaine qui ne gestoit que son eaue toute claire, suyuant son naturel et pour euiter les batelaiges du temps iadis, auquel contre toute raison et en peruertissant le commun cours des choses establies par le souuerain Createur, aucuns se faysoyent sortir d'entre les Nymphes le vin tant blanc que rouge, sa Majesté Tres Crestienne se trouua droict deuant St Jaques de l'Hospital.

This looks like a jibe at the fountain spouting wine at the Rheims Entry, but the practice of supplying refreshment, usually claret and hypocras at this point, ceased after 1491.[51]

(c) The Arch Facing Saint Jacques de l'Hôpital (fol. 6)

It may be recalled that the hôpital de la Trinité, which was the headquarters of the Confrérie de la Passion and which had featured in earlier Entries, had no part in the 1549 ceremonial. The Arch, illustrated in the *livret*, was an elaborate structure, with more florid ornamentation than the Saint-Denis outer portal, and it was one of the highlights of the Entry. The figure of Gallia ("une Gaule") is seen in her historical perspective: she is crowned with three towers, representing the three parts of Gaul; but her abundance and prosperity will also be symbolized. Both faces of the Arch were decorated with double columns—a feature to be found in the Lyon Entry, but also on the mausoleum of Francis I; and the order employed is the Corinthian, which as Vitruvius states is associated with Flora and Proserpina, and therefore eminently suited to celebrate *Gallia fertilis;* later La Fontaine was to call the order "superbe et magnifique." Trouble is taken to mention the correct proportions of the bases to the columns as well as the fluting. Here again, Serlio provides useful hints: the term used by him in Book I (on geometry) was "superbipartiens tertias," to define the area of the base of the columns: it reappears in the *Registres* (172) as "les piedestalz auuoyent proportion superbiparciente les tierces." Serlio prescribes the *cannelure* rising to the height of a third of a column. In his view, the Corinthian order, often highly ornate, is entirely appropriate for triumphal arches in Entries organized in honor of "alcun gran personnaggio"; such arches are, in addition, commonly graced by various paintings (as in this Entry). He explains that the column comprises nine parts, including the capital and the base;[52] the *livret,* excluding these two, refers to seven. The *Registres* (172) report that this arch, for all its splendor, was erected in an unexpectedly short time:

> . . . le myeulx conduict et entendu que jamais on en veid en
> France, pour le petit espace de temps que son architecte eut à le
> composer; et quant l'on diroit qu'un second Vitruve l'eust volon-
> tiers advoué pour son oeuvre, en quoy l'on ne penseroit faillir, à
> raison que toutes les proportions et beaultez artificielles y furent si
> bien observées qu'il estoit hors tous dangiers de calompnies.

But as we have seen, Alberti played his part here too. On the frieze
the mask and fleurons appear to have excited admiration; and the vault
of the arch was decorated by "un compartiment de moresque à grosses
rosaces d'or," which reflects contemporary interest in arabesque
tracery. The "feston de Lyerre" had a chiefly decorative intent, but the
more learned bystanders might have noted the plant's connection with
Bacchus and wine — relevant to *Gallia fertilis*. On either side of the in-
ner arch there were symbolic paintings of the two rivers Seine and
Marne, which the *livret* tells us were executed by the same artist. On
the arch were stationed the musicians who received special payment for
their performance (C, fol. 84). It was traditional to provide music at
this station; earlier the Porte aux peintres had stood here, but it was
destroyed in the 1530s and, for the present Entry, the municipality
decided to erect this triumphal arch on the old site.[53]

(d) The Obelisk or Aiguille du Sepulchre (fol. 9v)

This feature is also styled "piramide" in the *Comptes*. Though this is
one of the elements where the *Songe de Poliphile* counts for something,
the obelisk is well established in the minds of antiquarians as linked
with Roman triumphs. On its top there stands France in the guise of
Bellona, who addresses the monarch; and Bryant suggests that the
sides of the trigon may have concerned nobility, Parlement and
clergy.[54] The *Comptes* (fol. 55) add the picturesque detail that

> . . . y auoit faict dedans une forme de montée pour monter au
> hault d'icelle et aussi la charpenterie necessaire pour ayder à faire
> la forme de ladicte beste qui estoit sous ladicte obelisque.

The symbolism of the obelisk will be discussed later, but it is worth
noting that the presence of hieroglyphs had its classical precedents; as
Serlio recalls, there was an obelisk,

fuori di porta Capena nel circo, & e tutto sculpito di bizarrerie Egitte.[55]

(e) The Fontaine des Innocents (fol. 11v)

Originally this emplacement had been the *Fripiers'* accustomed station; but Henri II had abolished all guild productions shortly before, which left the way open for something new. According to Corrozet

> L'an mil cinq cens cinquante (*sic*) les fontaines S. Innocent furent basties de neuf, avec un corps d'hostel par dessus, le tout de pierre entaillée à l'antique, où sont representees au naturel les Nymphes & dieux Poëtiques, sur deux desquelles estant demy nues est escrit en lettres d'or: *Fontium Nymphis.*[56]

This feature, under construction for some time before, was opened on 16 June to coincide with and form part of the Royal ceremonies. Though we are not in the presence of a triumphal arch, Goujon's most recent biographer detects in it the lineaments of such a one, minus its plinth, and compares it with one of Serlio's models in Book IV.[57] Earlier antiquarians have suggested Goujon's hand in the design of this fountain and Pierre L'Escot may also have been involved.[58] The *livret* refers expressly to various "damoiselles & bourgeoises" and "gentils hommes & citoyens de la ville" stationed within the structure.

(f) The "Perspective" Facing the Châtelet (fol. 11v)

To honor Lutetia, the organizers devised a "portique à la mode Ionique," and this order, sacred to Juno and Diana (as well to the less masculine gods) was perhaps the most appropriate. The design was elaborate ("dipterique c'est à dire garnie d'ailes, ou double reng de colonnes"), with four pairs of columns supporting the façade, each pair repeated in depth, so that there were sixteen pairs altogether. The *livret* draws attention to the "pierre de meslange" used for the surface of the columns and this is not the only occasion on which the materials used are mentioned. However, the main accent lay on the *trompe-l'oeil* effect of the "perspective," brought about not only by the disposition and proportions of the columns, but by the gallery "percée à jour" which was intended to give an impression of solidity to the whole fabric. There are reasonable grounds for thinking that Jehan Cousin had the major say in this feature. Maurice Roy has suggested some parallels between the motif of this structure, *Lutetia nova Pandora,* and one of his paintings *Eva prima Pandora,* though the details of the two representations are hardly similar.[59] Perhaps more cogently, Panofsky has pointed to the Renaissance theme of *Roma prima Pandora* and to the creation of a Pandora shorn of her evil associations.[60] In this context, she would be seen then as a variation on the theme of abundance; moreover, her vessel (Pandora's box was unknown before the sixteenth century) would be linked with the quality of curiosity, seen as a virtue rather than as a defect — as for instance in the quest for learning. Nonetheless, one must not discount here the almost obsessive interest taken by Cousin in problems of perspective: in the book published in 1560 he devotes much space to the matter of perspective in the representation of the five orders, and there is a picture of a façade with six columns in which the problems of reduction according to the rules of perspective are studied.[61] In the Entry the figure of Lutetia is used as the point of focus, and for the same reason the steps leading up to the portico formed an integral part of the design.

(g) The First Arch of the Pont Notre-Dame (fol. 13v)

In earlier times, the procession had made its way to Notre-Dame by the Pont au Change; but for the entry of Eleanor of Austria Francis I had ordered that two arches be constructed on the Pont Notre-Dame to which the cortege was diverted. The same policy was adopted for the 1549 Entry. This arch was "de l'ordre composé," without columns but with niches in which some Argonauts were placed; the *Registres* (176) are more precise than the *livret* and say that the mouldings were "convenables à sa mode, cinquiesme en l'ordre des bastimens." Here we have another hint of the influence of Serlio who described this fifth order in addition to those found in Vitruvius: it is essentially a mixture of Ionic and Corinthian, and Serlio considered it to be exceedingly rare "eccetto che archi triomphali."[62] Important though these architectural features are, the *livret* is more concerned with the massive figure of Typhis and the accompanying Argonauts, and leaves the reader to peruse the illustration.

(h) The Second Arch, at the Further End of the Pont Notre-Dame (fol. 16v)

It was on the bridge itself that the procession waited while the King was at Notre-Dame. One will note the ideogram in which the initials of Henri and Diane de Poitiers are intertwined. The King's mistress was not forgotten in the pageant of the Entry.[63] The arch is not fully illustrated in the *livret,* because architecturally it was similar to the previous one. What was different were the figures: four archers, the King in the guise of *Genius Princeps,* Iris, the two Loves, Phoebus and Phoebe. The paintings, in the places corresponding to those of Phryxus and Helle in the previous arch, portrayed Aurora and Hesperus; they were meant to entertain those present while the King was in Notre-Dame.

(i) The Arch in front of the Palais (fol. 27v)

After the ceremony in Notre-Dame, the King went to the Palais de Justice by way of the rue de la Calandre, where there stood another triumphal arch, the description of which in the *livret* is complemented by an illustration. This was a double arch, and centrally placed in front was a figure of Minerva; the organizers used the Corinthian order for this feature, rather unexpectedly in view of what Du Choul has to say on the matter; but other considerations were also in play. Two Harpies carried perfumed torches, which classical antiquity connected with Aurora or Ceres—and here Minerva, as we noticed, combines the motifs of abundance and learning, though even learned contemporaries did not always grasp the symbolism: Corrozet thought the statue represented Venus.[64] The two nymphs symbolized Victory, Fame and Felicity. The lower third of the columns bore a leaf motif; and the system of steps within the arch was probably designed as part of the "perspective," affording a sense of breadth and depth, but also focussing the attention of the spectators on the figure of Minerva herself. She stood on three books, symbolic of her learning and prudence; and in her right hand, the fruits signified the benefits that would accrue to those who had served his Majesty properly.

(j) The Triumphal Arch near Saint-Paul in the Rue Saint-Antoine (fol. 36)

This arch did not form part of the processional route to Notre-Dame but was conceived as a form of entrance to the tourney in the rue Saint-Antoine. Described as Doric, it was thus military in inspiration, reinforced by the various figures adorning the structure. The striking feature, in honor of the King, is the H-shaped design, in which the artists have departed from precedent; but, with the "trophées ou despouilles antiques" decorating the arch, there is a blend of the "triumphateur" theme and the features suitable to the jousting which was to take place here. As on other occasions, the crescent and royal colors are prominently displayed — and the statues of the Gauls Brennus and Belgius, victors of Rome, form a pendant to the theme of Hercules. The representation of these two heroes on horseback reminds us of the accent laid on horsemen in the Entry — e.g. the Enfants de Paris, one of whom forms the subject of a plate in the *livret,* which may have been inspired in part by the picture — a splendid one — of the horseman in the Lyon *livret.* Henri II was not only very fond of hunting and riding, he also harked back to a chivalric conception of life. At the same time, the figures of Brennus and Belgius gave ample scope to the sculptors to show off their talents in neo-classical poses ("de si belle sculpture que les antiques se feussent contentez d'auoir faict aussi bien"). Charles le Conte was in charge of the carpentry for this arch — the bill which included other items came to 2900 l.t. — and the painting was entrusted to Cousin and Dorigny; Goujon is mentioned together with them for this work, but he may very well have been responsible for the sculptures (C, fol. 101 ff. and 108r-v).

(k) The Arch in the Rue Saint-Antoine near the "Coing des Tournelles" (fol. 38v)

The *livret* has little to say about this arch, made up of the main, central arch, flanked by two smaller ones; but a large illustration in the form of a *dépliant* is supplied. The square columns are what contemporaries called "attiques"; the military and jousting motifs are very much to the fore, not only in the statues in front of the structures, but in the two paintings above the lateral arches. It is not easy to make out what the paintings in the arches represent: one certainly suggests Fortune with her sail, and the figure in the left-hand arch has a distinct resemblance to Cousin's *Eva prima Pandora*. What is unusual — and the *livret* draws attention to this feature — is that on the top of the arch itself has been erected "une salle à la mode Françoise," that is, not in one of the classical orders. The *Comptes* do not refer to this structure, for the good reason that the City was not financially involved; but some notarial documents have come to light which, though the terminology used is not quite the same as in the *livret* and clear reference to our structure is not made, do seem to be relevant.[65] Philibert de l'Orme was instructed to erect a "grande salle" in the grounds of the hôtel des Tournelles for banquets and other entertainments: it was a sort of hangar made of wood, in principle, and 40 metres long by 3.30 metres wide. On 18 May de l'Orme negotiated the transfer of the carpentry work to Jehan and Leonard Fontaine, father and son. Jehan Rondel, already involved in the decoration of the hôtel de Graville, was entrusted with the painting and decoration of this "salle" for the sum of 200 écus d'or. On 20 June, the same painter, together with Baptiste Pellerin, was commissioned to provide further paintings for the structure, in front of the King's dais, and also other decorations including "figures de bronze de six pieds et histoires." It seems therefore highly probable that the design was worked out by Philibert de l'Orme who, for all his knowledge of classical architecture and his religious interpretations, wrote: "il est permis à l'exemple des anciens, d'inuenter & faire nouuelles colonnes";[66] the curious blend of styles displayed on this "salle" would be in line with his thinking.

Thus the Entry shows a certain thematic progression in the choice of architectural styles and orders, with the themes of Abundance and Fortune flanked by military prowess and strength. Conceived along neoclassical and "naturalist" lines, it is also enriched by a complex network of symbolism. Before we examine the exploitation of classical and other artistic sources not yet taken into account, something should be said about the impact of local politics on the Entry.

(VIII) The Entry as Expression of the Relations between King and City

Entries serve a multiplicity of purposes: we have noted briefly the importance of the 1549 Entry in the context of the rivalry between the Valois and the Hapsburgs, and there are unambiguous signs that religious dissidence will not be tolerated in the country. However, all Entries must also be concerned with the relations that develop between the King and the City into which he makes his Entry: usually the hope is expressed that the policies and privileges of the past will not be thrown overboard, that a body of acquired rights will continue to be recognized and that a promising future lies ahead under the wise leadership of the new King. However, the relations between Henri II and the municipality soon ran into trouble, as the inordinate delays show. Soon after his accession the Councillors had asked the King to cancel the levy of 40,000 l.t. imposed by Francis I shortly before his death. On the other hand, Henri II wished to increase pressure on the City: he hoped to extract more money from its coffers, and also wanted a gift of 300,000 l.t., which, as Bryant points out, was half the sum to be exacted from the nation as a whole, and also marks a shift towards royal privilege so far as the principles underlying the accessional gift are concerned.[67] Since the Entry ceremonial traditionally involved confirmation of municipal privileges, the delays encountered were tantamount to a refusal of recognition. Of course, agreement could not be deferred indefinitely, and the Entry expresses the hope that, broadly speaking, the policies of Francis I will be maintained and that the prosperous future of the country will be assured, by peaceful means if possible; nevertheless, the Entry reveals here and there more than a trace of the underlying tensions.

For instance, the harangues of both the first President of the Parlement and the Prévôt des Marchands reminded the King of his traditional duties and of his obligation to maintain the rights of the corporations and other interested parties. It may be that Lutetia's vessel (likened to Pandora's box) is a discreet symbolic hint that the capital's privileges should be maintained; and the obelisk, as we shall see, informs the king, by means of hieroglyphs, of its conception of the ideal Monarch. The status of various bodies or estates is not entirely stable, and this is reflected in the ceremonial. For instance, the traditional functions of the guilds tend to be eroded as the century wears on: the process was under way in the reign of Francis I who had refused the guilds permission to set up shows and plays for the 1531 Entry. In 1548, Henri II had forbidden the performance of mystery plays in the capital, and guildsmen did not perform separately in the Entry—thus there were no *tableaux vivants* in the rue Saint-Denis.

Another symptom is that the ceremony at Notre-Dame loses some of its significance; not that the religious side of the ceremonial is as it were downgraded, for the clergy are more heavily involved in the Entry in other ways. Indeed, there is quite a lot of reference to the Estates. The symbolism of the Fontaine du Ponceau with its figures of Jupiter and the three Fortunes, who represent the three Estates, is important in this context: they are seen to be working in harmony under the aegis of an enlightened leader. We have seen that the obelisk may also provide symbolic reference to the Estates, though we have insufficient evidence to be quite sure; and the Pont Notre-Dame decorations underline the importance of the nobility. Of course, this is a period when the status of the nobleman is shifting, through economic difficulties, the encroachment of central authority on his local privileges, and the growing importance of the Court, now less peripatetic than in the past, and therefore acting as more of a magnet to the nobility. All this is probably not implied in the symbolism, but the role of the nobility is reaffirmed with some vigor. More significant, no doubt, is the status of the Parlement. This is no new phenomenon: over a long period of time, the parlementarians had had the ambition to have a greater say in the ordering of things, and though one of the King's traditional functions was the dispensing of Justice, the Parlement came more and more to see itself as the perpetual guardian of the laws of the land. In his speech to Henri II, the first President had insisted on Parlement's duty to maintain justice and on certain other matters as well. In the sixteenth century the role of the officers of the Law continues to grow, especially as an arm of central authority, and in consequence the Parlements become, if not an Estate, at least one of the most powerful bodies in the realm. It is against this background that the symbolism of the arch in front of the Palais de Justice must be seen: Minerva, the goddess of wisdom becomes a symbol of the Law.

None the less, the Entry also reflects the increasing authority of the King: this is shown not only in the way he is presented as the unifying force in the country, but also by the emphasis laid on dynastic considerations. This appears both in the major presence of figures like Hercules, Typhis, Jupiter even, and in the symbolism of *Gallia fertilis.* Traditionally, this was the station associated with the Queen; the reduction of her presence redounds to the profit of the Monarch, and in the wider context of France. Kingly symbolism will be found on a broad scale throughout the Entry. Thus, much is made of Henri II's motto and crescent: he had adopted them when he was still Dauphin, and the motto *Donec totum impleat orbem,* probably inspired by Ovid, *Metamorphoses* XII, 617, "at vivit totum quae gloria compleat orbem," was displayed on the first triumphal arch. Claude Paradin wrote, apropos of the King's motto, that "es sacrées escritures donques, la Lune praefigure l'Eglise";[68] but perhaps more relevant is the interpretation of the crescent as a symbol of hope for the future. At the same time, the crescent suggests Diana—and therefore Diane de Poitiers: this is not the only reference to the King's favorite. Then there is the symbolism of the rhinoceros on which the obelisk is poised. The *Songe de Poliphile* has an illustration of an obelisk supported by an elephant: one can imagine that the planners were both influenced by the treatment of the motif in the *Songe* and anxious to avoid obvious imitation; but why the rhinoceros as a substitute? Gébelin's view was that the rhinoceros had been taken from an engraving of Enea Vico, 1542, representing the famous animal of Lisbon, but this may be far-fetched.[69] It seems that a rhinoceros was disembarked at Rotterdam in 1547, but this was a *fait divers* void of symbolism. The elephant is associated with chastity, piety and strength, but more important, it can be defeated only by the rhinoceros which, slow to anger, is invincible once roused; the latter trait would harmonize very well with the general symbolic pattern of the Entry. There is however the additional point that the rhinoceros was the device of duke Alexander of Medici, with the motto "non velvo sin vencer," which Giovio and Symeoni gloss "Rhinoceros numquam victus ab hoste redit."[70] In the context of the conflict between Henri II and the Emperor Charles V this would be entirely appropriate. There are other, minor examples of royal symbolism, such as the reference to the "cordeliere" (fol. 28) which, adopted as an emblem by Anne of Brittany, descended to Louise de Savoie; one may also wonder whether the association of Flora and the lily is not also a discreet allusion to the Queen's Florentine antecedents. Difficulties of interpretation may arise because the symbolism is often polyvalent and highly erudite; even learned contemporaries misunderstood certain features of the Entry, and it is not easy to keep a steady line between failure to detect references and an overenthusiastic pursuit of the eccentric.

However, there is no doubt that, though the Entry takes into account the tensions and strains of the relations between the King and various bodies, the Entry encourages the glorification of Kingship in an increasingly centralized economy; and with this apotheosis we are well on the way to the stage where the Roi Soleil sits on the throne basking in the principle of Divine Right.

(IX) Further Humanist Themes and Symbolism

The concept of the Entry as symbol or allegory is of course fundamental to such a form of ritual; what however seems new in the Paris

Entry of 1549 is, on the one hand, the greater attempt made at systematic symbolism and, on the other, the vigorous exploitation of newer, humanist sources which the *livret* often feels obliged to elucidate in some detail. Over and above the direct use of classical mythology — sometimes modified by humanist myth or deliberately transferred for thematic reasons — there are humanist sources which were becoming more widely familiar and which were known in particular to one of the organizers — Jean Martin. Here a variety of strands seem to come together opportunely: the emerging taste for veiled truths, the mixture of literary text and visual arts, the developing links between the emblem, conceived along pedagogic lines, and the enthusiasm with which princes and noble families interest themselves in *imprese*, the desire to loosen certain bonds with the medieval past, the relations between architectural motifs and symbolism, all these concerns contribute to the presence of such extensive symbolism in the Entry.

Jean Martin, in addition to his being extremely interested in the potentiality of classical architecture, was an enthusiast for symbolic utterance. As early as 1543 he had translated Horus Apollo; and he cannot have been insensitive to the extraordinary vogue of Alciat's Emblems.

(a) Alciat's work may well be a possible source of symbols. After all, the *Emblemata* offered on a small scale a formula that is exploited more broadly in the ceremonies: mottoes, symbolic features, gnomic verse, veiling of truth from the uneducated. Naturally there are points where such a source would overlap with others, but the immense popularity of the Emblems must have affected the organizers too. We have seen that a possible origin for the friendly relations between Virtue and Fortune was to be found in Alciat;[71] but there are other themes relevant to the Entry. Such are: *Concordia* (pp. 8 and 29) and even more pertinently *Ex pace ubertas* (p. 21), the theme of the two Loves, Cupid and Anteros (pp. 75 and 84), mentioned in the *livret* (fol. 16) with an allusion to its classical origin, Plato *Bonus eventus* is the subject of an emblem (p. 81), though the treatment is admittedly different from that in the Entry; then there is *Janus Bifrons*, used as a symbol of prudence in connection with Louis XII on the present from the City to the King; and there are mythological heroes or beasts found in both Alciat and the Entry: Phryxus on the ram (p. 90), Hercules depicting *Eloquentia fortitudine praestantior* (p. 86) and the motto *Bonis a diuitibus nihil timendum* (p. 105), illustrated by Phineas, the Harpies, Calais and Zethes. At the very least one can see that the organizers of the Entry were building on themes that had become the common currency of humanism.

(b) The *hieroglyphic tradition*, as represented by Horus Apollo. This accounts for the introduction of the obelisk in one sense, since it bears "un grand quarré contenant les veuz des Parisiens en hieroglyphes" (*livret*, fol. 10r–v). There were other precedents: Alberti talks of the meaning of various hieroglyphs,[72] the obelisk was long since associated with triumphs, the *Songe de Poliphile* had introduced it, and above all there was the stimulus of the Lyon Entry which had

> Une haulte obelisque en forme de Piramide quarrée de soixante troys piedz & plus de haulteur, le pedestal de douze taillé à la rustique, aux deux frontz duquel estoit escript *Nomen qui terminat astris*.[73]

When it came to preparing a list of the "veuz des Parisiens," it seems that Martin must have drawn primarily on Horus Apollo for the symbolism of the motifs selected. Some ideograms are elucidated in the *livret*; others are telescoped or omitted.

The lion and the dog resting on the crown maintain the traditional meanings of Fortune and Vigilance respectively (the Lion does not appear in Horus Apollo in this context). The *livre antique* has an omnibus value in the Renaissance to cover poetry, reputation, philosophy, wisdom, justice, but the *livret* favors the interpretation *conseil*. The naked sword that transfixes the book is understood in the text as *bonne expedition*, though this would appear to be a very rare symbol.[74] The twisted or coiled serpent, on the other hand, is the normal symbol for Prudence. The "globe ou marchepied" is simply the Earth, though there are associations with justice and fame; and "une poupe de nauire & un trident" are explained in the text as dominion over the sea. The open eye, almost certainly taken from Horus Apollo, stands for the eye of justice, but also for the presence of God. "Unes fasces consulaires" would seem to refer to the defence of the realm; the "rond en cercle" which Tervarent traces back to the *Songe de Poliphile*,[75] means "tousiours," as the *livret* informs us; the "pavois" defined by Cotgrave as a "great shield or target," has in all likelihood meanings similar to those claimed by "bouclier" in Tervarent's inventory, and in particular Fortitude.[76] The "ancre de long," which likewise features in the *Songe*, may be connected with the dolphin: it was the device adopted by Augustus. Aldus Manutius took it over as part of his device and its meaning was expounded by Erasmus in his *Adagia*. In antiquity it was a ready symbol for security and support. The two hands clasped over olive branches stand for the promise of good faith; the cornucopia turns up yet again, while the deer, the companion of Diana, is often an attribute of Prudence, which is stressed more than once in the Entry as a kingly quality. The dolphin is connected with Fortune and the meaning of the laurel needs no comment; but the "lampe antique allumée" is more cryptic: it occurs in the *Songe* together with a rudder and an olive branch, so that it seems to harmonize the virtues of Charity and Vigilance.[77] According to Tervarent, the horse's bit refers primarily to Temperance;[78] the helm of a ship (tying in with the symbol of the City of Paris) denotes two attributes that appear prominently in the Entry, Abundance and Fortune. So that what we are offered in these hieroglyphs is a *Miroir des Princes*, expressing the virtues which the City would wish to find in the ideal Monarch; and they often underline motifs found elsewhere in the Entry. Here and there we come across symbols not always elucidated: thus on fol. 15v reference is made to "arcs à corde rompue." One may wonder at the repeated presence of the Harpies, though this could be explained partly by reference to the *Songe*. On the other hand, the description of Aurora (*livret*, fol. 17) clarifies both the "teste de boeuf seiche," which means "labeur," and the "lampe allumée" denoting the "lumiere du jour approchante de nostre hemisphere," but it is worth noting that these two symbols appear in succession in Horus Apollo.[79] The association of trumpet and fame is exploited on fol. 28 of the *livret*, though not perhaps as vigorously as some motifs we have come across; and the Entry can be seen as a series of variations on *Renommée* and success. On the same page, the vases stand for "perpetuelle felicité," but they are variously attributes of Pandora, Nemesis, and Fortune.

(c) *Mottoes and Inscriptions*. These appear to be exploited beyond anything found in previous Entries. Once again we are faced with a concourse of sources. At one level, it is evident that the use of inscriptions imparts a further neoclassical flavor to the Entry; for some time antiquarians and humanists had been taking an interest in epitaphs, epigraphs, coins and medallions furnished with inscriptions. No doubt this trend does not gain full momentum until a bit later—Du Choul's famous treatise on the religion of the Romans had yet to come out —but numismatic activity was commmon enough among the more scholarly. Epigraphs had been described and quoted at length by Italian antiquaries and historians; nor is it a coincidence that the collector of *imprese* Gabriele Symeoni had collected coins during the early 1550's. The passion for *imprese* was on the increase among princely families, a passion no doubt reinforced by the success of the Emblems.

All this contributes to the use of mottoes and inscriptions which the occasion and the medium must perforce reduce to manageable proportions. Most of these are in Latin, so far as the Paris Entry is concerned,
but there are quatrains in the vernacular, provided for the less erudite,
one assumes. These formulae serve partly to epitomize in mnemonic or
convenient form the essence of some motif, partly to emphasize the
neo-classical character of the Entry, partly in consequence to flatter by
adroit comparison with the celebrities of the Roman Empire and the
classical world.

A certain number of these formulae are taken from or inspired by
classical authors, and in particular Vergil. The first motto following the
King's is "trahimur, sequimurque volentes"; as the *livret* points out, it is
a "hemistiche, certes," and if it is not in fact a poetic echo, it reminds us
forcibly of Cicero, *De officiis*, i, 6, 8: "omnes trahimur et ducimur ad
cognitionis et scientiae cupiditatem." The next formula is Vergilian
(fol. 3v), "Adgredere o magnos (aderit iam tempus) honores," *Eclogue*,
IV, 48 being the original. On fol. 5v "Sors fida potentum" may be invented, but the genitive form of *potens* and the use of that case after *fida*
are both rare and found in the last book of the *Aeneid*.   More than a
Vergilian echo is perceptible in "Tibi sceptra Iouemque conciliant"; [80]
and the elegiac couplet

> Terra antiqua, potens armis, atque ubere glebae,
>   Terna tibi populo Gallia mater alo

owes its hexameter to *Aeneid*, I, 531. Later a borrowing from Vergil is
acknowledged:

> Alter erit iam Typhis, & altera quae vehat Argo
> Delectos heroas   (*Eclogue,* IV, 34–35)

and the inscription relating to Henri II on the gift made to him by the
City has Horatian ancestry ("Tumidis velis Aquilone secundo": cf.
Epist. I, ii, 201). "A me principium" (fol. 17) might be an echo of "A
Ioue principium" (Vergil, *Eclogue*, III, 60). Occasionally a motto uses a
word in a poetic sense (*nepotes*, fol. 36v meaning "descendants") and one
or two formulae are indebted to the Roman historians: thus the iden-
tification of Dis with the Celtic god of night goes back to Caesar, *B. G.*,
6, 18, 1 ff. Only a few lines of Latin verse appear to be original, while
the inscriptions maintain a conventional style in keeping with their re-
quirements. One unusual feature is the use of a Homeric tag (fol. 14),

which for that reason the author of the *livret* feels constrained to render into French. He had already introduced the Greek epithet ἀλεξίκακος,[81] and here again a French equivalent has been provided: "qui vault autant à dire comme en domtant les monstres, ou mauvais" (Liddell and Scott say, more precisely, "warding off mischief "). The epithet is applied, in Greek literature, both to Mercury and here more relevantly to Hercules, to whom the late King had been likened.

The more scholarly allusions and echoes needed some vernacular counterbalancing, and a number of inscriptions were introduced in French, though they were set in "cartoches antiques." The quatrains are not numbered in the original text. The first (fol. 3v, for the first triumphal arch) is put in the mouth of Francis I represented as Hercules and takes as its starting point the notorious chains of eloquence; the reader is invited to follow the new King "contrainct de franche volunté," as faithfully as he did his predecessor, so that the theme of eloquence is given a political twist. The *Registres* (171) add a comment omitted in the *livret* to the effect that the second distich is "à la louenge du Roy Henry, triumphateur." Quatrain II (fol. 5), inscribed on the Fontaine du Ponceau, contrasts a "Grand Romain" (Caesar or Augustus have been suggested) and his "sort fatal" with the happier predicament of a new monarch favored by Fortune and God. The theme of *Gallia fertilis* inspires two quatrains (fol. 8v): III, like that on the fountain, exploits an antithesis between Roman antiquity and France, and a similar pattern occurs in IV with a comparison between Flora and Henri II as harbingers of prosperity. On fol. 10v, Quatrain V compares Henri and Hercules as conquerors, while VI (on the "perspective") states the parallel between Pandora, receiving gifts from the gods of yore, and Lutetia, offered to the new King. VII likens the Argo to Henri's ship of state (fol. 14v), while VIII (fol. 17v) on the further arch of the Pont Notre-Dame sees in the great concourse of gods and demigods proof of the King's claims to be the greatest of all victors. The final quatrain (IX), concerning the H-shaped arch, establishes a flattering contrast between the victories of the two Gaulish leaders and Henri's triumphant future in his domination of "les plus fins & plus forts."

The French quatrains, intended to emphasize the leitmotif of the Entry for the crowds, point to the prosperity of France, the need for obedience, and above all the presence of the "Roy triumphateur." The military, aggressive element of the ceremonies is made abundantly clear. So far as the literary qualities of these verses are concerned, little need be said: they are, for the most part constructed on a simple antithesis between Roman past and French present and future. Scholars have asked themselves who was or were the author(s); the quatrains reveal no poetic personality and they could have been written by any of the current poetasters, François Habert, Gilles Corrozet or, as is much more likely, the two men involved in organizing the ceremonies, Thomas Sebillet and Jean Martin. The odds are on Sebillet, in view of his own poetic activity, but one did not need to be poet to produce these Christmas cracker trifles.[82]

(x) Linguistic Aspects of the *livret*

Jean Martin was essentially a translator; in the *Registres* (170) there is an important passage, almost certainly from his pen, on the cultural achievements of Francis I's reign, not only in literature and learning, but also in

> . . . mesmement la langue françoise qui par avant estoit assez champestre: mais au moyen des bons ars et sciences qui luy ont esté communiquez par la dilligence de ce bon Roy, non iamais assez louable, elle s'est tant enrichie de termes propres et signifficatiz que maintenant luy est loisible de dire tout ce que bon luy semble en quelque matiere que ce soit, aussi nayvement que aucune des modernes.

Clearly Martin felt that he had contributed to this happy state of affairs by his activity as a translator. One curious consequence of the attitude expressed in the *Registres* is that the *livret* becomes an extremely interesting linguistic document.

It is not that the *livret* contains a great number of words appearing in print for the first time; in any case, one must always be careful in this area, as is shown by a comparison between the datings for neologisms given in the first edition of Dauzat's *Dictionnaire étymologique* and those of the second edition. On the evidence of the first edition, the *livret* would give the impression of a highly original text, but recent research has altered the picture drastically, and doubtless more work would further change the picture. However, a sizeable number of technical words in this text may have appeared for the first time in Jean Martin's translations. What is interesting about the *livret* is the high concentration of technical terms of recent vintage which are being taken beyond the confines of the specialist. Some words likely to prove unfamiliar may be explained in the *livret* (e.g. *stilobate*, first dating 1547), and occasionally a more elaborate technical phrase may be omitted, though it is to be found in the *Registres*. Among the more recent words we note: *capperassonnée* (BW 1546), *caraquin*(BW 1546), *cartoche* (BW 1547), *compartiment* (BW 1546), *distique* (BW 1548), *hemicycle* (BW 1547), *rez-de-chaussée* (as noun BW 1548), *rudentée* (D 1551). Certain other terms appear with much later datings in the etymological dictionaries: *bronzé* (BW c. 1560), *frizons* (BW 1574), *hieroglyphe* (BW 1576). A number of terms not mentioned by D or BW occur in the *livret*: *billetté, contredos, diagoné* (found later in Cotgrave), *dipterique* (from Vitruvius and explained in the text), *emulateur* (later in Cotgrave), *hydrie, lacunaire* (noun), *pancarpe, pegme, sode, spatiosité* (also in Martin's Serlio), *topiaire, trigone* (taken no doubt from Vitruvius). We come across a few words that may have turned up at an earlier date but in a different form. The zeal of the *Registres* may be curbed in the *livret* which, for instance, does not print: "les piedestalz avoyent proportion superbiparciente les tierces (a calque from Serlio), c'est a dire estoyent justement . . . " (172); or "rapportées en vraye equidistance triangulaire, brunyes et resplendissantes à merveille contre le soleil" (173); and a simpler formula may be substituted: "menez par practique de perspective" (176) makes way for "menez par industrie" (fol. 12). Against this, one may find a preference for the more learned, but also more precise word: thus *tableau* and *cartoche* are both used, but the learned term appears first in the text and on fol. 14v *cartoche* is preferred to *tableau* which occurs in the *Registres*; on fol. 15v *flou* disappears in the *livret* in favor of *entremeslé;* and *pendoient à niveau* is replaced by *à plomb de son centre* (fol. 17). Generally speaking, the *Registres* are rather more prolix and like to indulge themselves: on fol. 2v, 11, 13–14 we are spared, after *chapiteaux*, "garnys de frize, armilles, balancier, astragalle ou talus, plinte, doulcine et tallouer" (R, 168). Of course, the *livret*'s search for greater concision would be determined by economic considerations, the need to be more accessible to the average reader, the superfluity of description in the presence of good illustrations—the *livret*, like that of the Lyons Entry, reflects the increasing recognition of the value of "visual aids" and of the technical improvements that are being developed in the printing trade. There are none the less passages in the *Registres,* omitted in the *livret*, that tell us much about the cultural concerns of the organizers: we have mentioned Germain Boursier's observations on the Hercules legend and the comments on the French language; others are less substantial, but not without interest, such as the additional remarks on the resemblance of Typhis to Henri II:

dont le visage (*livret*: "la figure") approchoit fort des lineamens
physionomiques du Roy triumphateur, et tant bien formé de tous
membres que Phidias et Praxiteles n'y eussent trouvé à redire.
(R, 176)

Finally there are divergences between the *Registres* and the *livret* of a
grammatical nature (genders, prepositions, choice between the older
and the newer word or form: e.g. *dextre/droicte*, or *qui/lequel*); there are
signs in the *livret* of a search for greater syntactical precision. Clearly
some trouble has been taken in the *livret* to strike a balance between in-
novatory precision and a grim surfeit of neologisms. The *livret* can in
this sense be viewed as a prolongation of Jean Martin's efforts to make
the vernacular a satisfactory means of communicating technical information; and from his point of view the *Deffense et illustration de la
langue françoyse* would be little more than a glimpse of the obvious.

(xi) The Pléiade and the Entry

This brings us to the obvious question: were the members of the
Pléiade involved in the preparation of the Entry, and if not, why not?
At one time critics detected a certain parallelism between the neo-
classicism that informs the Entry and the attitudes expressed by
Joachim du Bellay in his *Deffense et illustration.* One can certainly see
how neo-classical principles harmonize with an acutely felt nationalism
in the cultural domain, which seeks ways and means of renewal
without sacrificing the essentials of the national heritage. Such a view is
tenable, with a few reservations. In the first place, there is no evidence
to show that the members of the Pléiade (or Brigade as the group was
called in the early days)[83] took the slightest part in a series of
ceremonies organized by men whose main interests lay in the field of
architecture and to a lesser extent in sculpture and painting; in any
case, an Entry will depend more on the visual than on the verbal and
literary for its effects. Secondly, where literary concerns are present, it
is equally clear that the Brigade were not in the running. Of course,
they were not yet properly established, and there are indeed grounds
for suspecting that the Entry hastened the publication of the *Deffense et
illustration* which received its privilège on 30 March 1549 and was to appear towards the end of the following month; but this was partly in
reaction against the threat posed by the fact that others had been

preferred in high quarters. It is at this point that the name of Thomas Sebillet enters the picture; he is mentioned in the *Comptes* (fol. 89v–90) in his capacity as "ingenieux" and he acted as a sort of lieutenant to Jean Martin. He had published his *Art poetique françoys* in 1548 and his selection in these circumstances must have induced in the Brigade a sense of disappointment, for though many of his ideas were similar to those of the *Deffense et illustration,* he had nailed his literary colors to the mast of the Marotic tradition. His more conservative outlook would surely appeal to Henri II whose court poet was after all a latter-day *rhétoriqueur,* François Habert. Still there is nothing to show that the King expressed an opinion on this matter; on the other hand a friend of the Pléiade, Michel de l'Hôpital, at that time a City councillor, must have concurred in Sebillet's appointment. There was some distance separating the organizers of the Entry and the younger poetic genera-tion — on the attitude to the cultural past, and also on the problems of the literary language. At the same time one must not exaggerate the differences: there is a substantial measure of overlap in the basic aesthetic principles, and subsequently, relations between some of these men became close. Sebillet got on very well with members of the Pléiade; and Jean Martin, to whom Ronsard, at the end of 1549, ad-dressed an ode,[84] is generally thought to be the author of the *Breve ex-position* which is placed at the end of the 1550 edition of the *Odes.*

Thwarted though the Brigade might feel at being excluded from the organization of the Entry, two members at least saw fit to make some contribution on the sidelines, in the hope of currying favor at Court; and their compositions came out before the Entry took place. One was Joachim du Bellay's *Prosphonématique* (i.e. address or harangue); no full copy of the first edition is at present known — the title page of the one copy available in a public library is missing; but Marty-Laveaux, who had the good fortune to see a complete copy a century ago, described the title page which referred to the Entry taking place on 14 June, the day fixed before the weather forced its postponement.[85] The text shows awareness of the nature of the preparations and this may have affected Du Bellay's treatment of the subject. He makes some play with the Hercules motif, stresses French culture and Henri II's military prow-ess, and develops themes of Nature: rustic Nature has its eyes on the King, and a fairly long passage is devoted to the Seine. Not vintage Du Bellay, rather opportunist verse. The other contribution came from Ronsard: his *Avant-entrée du roy treschrestien à Paris* may well, as Paul Laumonier suggested, have appeared in the first fortnight of June.[86] This composition, longer than Du Bellay's, differs especially in that the poet concentrates his attention more on Catherine de Médici and aligns himself with the Guises.

The poet who writes most in honor of the ceremonies is in fact Salmon Macrin, the Neo-Latin writer who had been *cubicularius regius* under Francis I and managed to retain his title under the new régime: his two books of *Epigrammata,* published in 1548, give the appearance of a man only too anxious to remain in favor with the new monarch. Knowing Henri II's attitude to his father and those the latter protected, Macrin could be forgiven his anxiety, and all the more as he had a numerous family to support; more serious, his religious outlook, though he seems to have remained orthodox, might seem suspect to the fanatical. He was a close friend of Ronsard and Du Bellay. He composed for the ceremonies three poems which were printed in his *Epitome.*[87] The first concerns the *sacre* at Rheims in 1547; the second was addressed to Catherine de Médici and develops the theme of the Golden Fleece, a subject which his friend Du Bellay was to exploit later. The last and most substantial poem is entitled "De Regis et reginarum ingressu in urbem Lutetiam": some of it is little more than a stylized description of the procession and, proportionately more space is given over to the King's praying at Notre-Dame. Mention is made of Marguerite de France, and indeed she and the Queen receive more attention than does the King.

All this does not add up to very much, and one must confess that the poetic aspects of the Entry are slight. After all, the Entry shows more interest in the visual arts, as one would expect; and it will be left to the Pléiade to give expression later to the literary aspirations of the times. One might ask oneself whether the Entry did not leave traces in the work of Ronsard: certain themes overlap, even though they flourish in the humanist climate of the times — Ulysses and the Argonauts, Hercules, Castor and Pollux, Calais and Zethe, *la France fertile,* mythological symbolism, perhaps even the transference of the idea of perspective into his own poetry. Obviously this can be no more than speculation, but it points to interesting areas of overlapping inspiration, and we know that Pierre de Ronsard was very sensitive to what the visual arts had to offer.

C. Postlude

(XII) The Tourney

The *livret* informs us that, after the Entry proper, the royal couple remained for a month in the Palais des Tournelles; and for some of this period the famous tourney was in progress. It was to be the last time on which a tourney formed part of the Paris Entry celebrations: the death of Henri II in a joust cast its shadow over subsequent Entries in this respect. As early as 1 April a proclamation was made to the effect that a tourney would be organized, and as Belleforest puts it:

> le premier iour d'Auril, audict an, il auoit par des Heraux d'armes fait publier par les carrefours de sadicte ville de Paris les articles du Tournoy, entrepris pour la sollennité de son tres-heureux couronnement & triomphante entrée, de luy, & la Royne, sa compagne, pour ouurir le pas d'iceluy au premier iour de Iuin . . . [88]

But, since the Entry had to be postponed, the tourney was in consequence put off until 23 June. The royal instructions for the necessary preparations were signed by the duc d'Aumale, the maréchal de la Marche "et autres tenans" (C, fol. 105v); and there was a great deal to do over and above the H-shaped arch and the "grande salle" near the Tournelles. According to Sauval, the area required in the rue Saint-Antoine stretched from the rue Saint-Paul right to the Bastille, and one of the major items was the removal of the paving stones from the rue Saint-Antoine.[89] The *Comptes* show the hiring of labor for this purpose from 15 April to 25 May and of course, when it was all over, workmen had to be found to repave the street.[90] Agreement was reached with Guillaume de Saint-Jorre — the "maistre pavier de grais" whose name turns up from time to time in the accounts and who will later be hired for paving the main court at Anet — to restore the street for the sum of 1697 l. 16 s. 4 d.t. (C, fol. 146). There was also levelling work undertaken on the area where the tourney was to take place (C, fol. 110). A contract was entered into with two "manoeuvriers et voicturiers par terre" on 25 May, but the main work seems to have been accomplished from 23 June to 6 July to maintain a satisfactory surface (C, fol. 110v–111). According to the contract of 3 April, Charles le Conte was involved in the construction of various "eschauffaults" or stands from which the jousting could be watched by the Queen, the umpires, the ambassadors, the Governor of Paris (at that time François de Montmorency) and his company, and there was also the "eschauffault de la Ville" (C, fol. 103v–104v). Major alterations had to be made to the Queen's stand "pour garder le soleil de frapper si fort dedans ledict eschauffault" (C, fol. 106v); the painting of the stand was undertaken by Jacques Conte and Martin Frelon (C, fol. 108).[91] Charles le Conte was furthermore responsible for the carpentry work of the H-shaped arch which acted as entrance to the tourney.

To entertain the company, when jousting was not in progress, provision was made for the "grande salle." All this was to be under the general supervision of Monsieur de Saint-Martin (i.e. Il Primaticcio) who had suffered some eclipse on the accession of Henri II and entered the service of the Guises in 1548. Apparently he had been responsible for showing courtiers to their places in the houses lining the Royal route.[92] In all this we may surely detect signs of the rivalry between the Montmorency and the Guise factions at court: whereas Montmorency and his friends have it more or less their own way in the Entry where the municipality of Paris is concerned, the Guises court the King in the organization of the jousting and naval combat, and appear at the same time to be more sympathetic to the talents of Italian artists resident in France, though here the distinction between Italian and French skills should not be exaggerated.

Belleforest provides an account of the tourney in which hyperbole and precise detail jostle one another:

> . . . & au long de la grand ruë Sainct Anthoine, estoient les lices magnifiquement dressées, faisans monstre de part & d'autre de deux grands arcs, precieusement & ingenieusement enrichis de deuices, auec statuës, & bordures par les costez des loges grandes & richement tapissées, où la Royne & les Dames, les iuges du Tournoy, & Ambassadeurs des Potentats voysins virent ouurir le pas audict Tournoy, le Dimenche vingt & troisiesme iour de Iuin audict an, par monseigneur François de Lorraine, Duc d'Aumale: le sire Robert de la Marche, Seigneur de Sedan, Mareschal de France: le sire Iaques d'Albon, Seigneur de Saint André, Mareschal de France: le sire Claude Gouffier, Seigneur de Boisy, grand Escuyer de France: sire Gaspard de Saulx, Seigneur de

Tavennes, Capitaine de cinquante hommes d'armes: & le sire Philibert de Marsilly, seigneur de Cipierre, Gentil-homme de la Chambre du Roy, les six tenans contre tous venans, tant François comme estrangers: & par le Roy, accompagné de trente hommes d'armes premier assaillant. En ce Tournoy fust procédé les quinze iours suyuans par monseigneur Anthoine de Bourbon, Duc de Vendosmois, & tous les autres Princes & Seigneurs consecutiuement assaillans, suyuant la forme des huict emprises, declarées au long par les articles du Tournoy: auquel les Princes & Gentils hommes de France, & singulierement la Maiesté du Roy, fist monstre & preuue suffisante de la vaillance, magnanimité & dexterité aux armes, tant à cheual comme à pied.[93]

On 2 July, the King in accordance with ancient custom went to the Palais ("dedans la Chambre dorée") where he dispensed Justice.

(XIII) The Naval Battle and the Storming of the Fort on the Ile de Louviers

On Wednesday 3 July, after dinner, the King and Queen set off the attend a naval combat on the Seine and "par une braue Gondole furent menez dedans le batteau que la Ville auoit faict dresser & enrichir de leurs couleurs."[94] The idea of such an entertainment appears to have taken shape comparatively late, since instructions were sent out from La Rocheguyon on 14 May for the City to make the necessary arrangements. All this was to involve the fortification of the Ile de Louviers, the construction of a harbor, the erection of boat bridges on the Ile aux Vaches and the Ile Notre-Dame, "pour venir assaillir ledict fort par esbatemens et pour plus grande magnificence desdictes entrees" (AN K 957 pièce 14). The *Comptes* (fol. 149v) mention that the program was "expressément commandé et ordonné par le roy." Two points arise here: on the one hand, the letters patent carried the signature of the duc d'Aumale on behalf of the King, as did the instructions for the arrangements for the tourney; and on the other hand, there is the question where the idea originated. Two sources suggest themselves: first, there had been a naval combat during the Lyon Entry in the previous year, and second, the birth of Louis, duc d'Orléans (3 February 1549) had been celebrated in highly successful fashion in Rome on 14 March, with an assault on a fort forming part of the program:

E vengo à la sostanza de la Festa, che fu di giostra, di stoccho à
cauallo, & a pié: di scaramuccia, d'assalti di fuochi, & de la presa
per forza d'un castello, fabricato su la porta del Palazzo di Santo
Apostolo, oue hora allogia il Reuerendiss. & Illustrissimo Cardinal di Bellay.[95]

An entertainment blending the formula of Lyon and Rome could
hardly fail to please the King or the citizens of Paris who had witnessed
a very grandiose Entry, but one in which traditional pastimes had been
somewhat reduced. The *livret* does not concern itself with the *naumachia,*
but contemporary witnesses considered it an impressive part of the
festivities; the *Comptes* provide detailed information on the preparations
and on certain items of special interest. First of all, labor was employed
on the fortifications of the Ile de Louviers, the building of the harbor
and the erection of a rampart from 3 June onwards (C, fol. 150). A
great deal of carpentry work was involved: in the course of one week
twenty carpenters were active, in another week there is mention of
seventy-two "autres manoeuvres," in yet another of sixty-two. Moreover men were hired to guard the sites and materials (C, fol. 159v); and
Clement Delaire, master joiner, received 45 l.t. for "ung croissant et
une fleur de lis à quatre fleurons le tout de boys de noix qui a esté mis
sur la tour estant au meillieu dudict fort" (C, fol. 164v). The oversight
of the construction of the fort was entrusted to Francisco Malacorda,
"Ingenieux depputé par le roy à dresser ledict fort" (C, fol. 175), a task
which took him thirty days. Charles Dorigny was in charge of the fort;
according to a contract signed on 28 June, he was to receive the sum of
160 l.t.

> . . . pour auoir faict et parfaict les ouuraiges à paincture dudict
> fort en lisle de louuiers, Ainsi qu'il s'ensuict. C'est assauoir painct
> les deux portes d'icelluy fort en facon de pierre rusticque et
> audessus de la premiere porte, painct deux figures tenans ung
> escu de france auec l'ordre et la couronne et plus hault une nature
> ayant les deux bras estenduz tenant en la main droicte unge fleur
> de liz et à l'autre ung croissant au costé droict de la nature,
> painctz hommes femmes et enffans de diuerses sortes et au costé
> senestre de toutes sortes de bestes sur lesquelles tumboit du lait
> tant d'un costé que d'autre des mammelles de ladicte nature. Item
> trois tables d'attente pour escripre la signification de ladicte
> histoire. Item a l'autre costé painct deux autres figures, l'une force
> et l'autre prudence tenant ung escu de france auec de (*sic*)

couronne et au-dessus une femme debout tenant en sa main droicte une couronne de laurier et en l'autre main une escorgée (i.e. thong), et audessoubz plusieurs gens beuuant et mengeant entre lesquelz y auoit ung ayant les yeux bendez en champ obscur et melincollique. Item au costé droict painct grant compagnie de gens auec estralabes, spheres, rigles, escarres, compas, lymes, Instrumens et plusieurs autres choses semblables, en champ cler et ioyeulx, et audessus trois tables d'attente pour escripre la signification de ladicte histoire; le tout faict sur toille et bonne paincture. Item painct les escussons et armoiries des six tenans sur tableaulx de boys, le tout de bonnes et unies coulleurs d'or et d'argent. Item painct tous les murs de rouge en facon de brique et les tours en facons de pierre de taille, les boullevers faictz en poinctes de diamant de gris blanc et noir, escarlatte en facon de pierre de taille. (C, 174r–v)

Dorigny must have had to work pretty fast, which did not prevent his being paid with considerable delay—on 13 December. The list of wooden material is large, but in addition there was the fitting out of the galleys due to take part in the assaults.

It was Charles le Conte who drew up the model of the galleys, and the reproduction of the replicas was entrusted to the well-known Francisque Scibec de Carpi, "menuisier du roi," who was active at Fontainebleau and in March 1549 was working at Anet under Philibert de l'Orme:[96] he was paid 990 écus soleils "pour auoir . . . faict et accomodé en forme de galleres trente trois basteaulx de diuerses longueurs" (C, fol. 175v). Three of the vessels were larger than the rest and were "garnies de panaizades et d'auirons a chacune dix, douze, seize et dixhuict et aussi esdictes poupe et proue ornemens en facon antique" (C, fol. 176). Scibec, for his part, contracted with two "charpentiers de bateaux" for the fabrication of 210 pairs of oars at 12 sols the pair,[97] though Thibault, one of the men concerned, subcontracted his share to Pierre Gohier. The oars, masts and other features were then painted for the sum of 594 1.t. by "Luc Penny," that is, Lucas Penni, known as Romain, who was active in the decoration of Fontainebleau and must have been a close friend of Scibec, since he made the latter one of the executors of his will.[98] Jacques Le Gros received 950 l.t. 4 s. 6 d.t. for the silk drapings used on the vessels and for the outfits of the "conducteurs d'icelles" (C, fol. 177); and Cornart Pynart was paid 149 l. 15 s.t. for "ung grant tendail de damas blanc pour tendre et couurir la pouppe de la galere appellee la cappitaineresse" (C, fol. 178), as well as for one or two sundries. Special and costly items were the "construction tant d'une salle faicte sur un grand basteau où le roy et la royne soupperoient le iour du combat naual que des eschauffaulx faictz le long des murs de la closture de ladicte ville viz a viz de la Riuiere où estoit ladicte dame pour icelluy combat veoir plus à son ayse et aussi d'une fueillée qui se debuoit faire en l'isle de Louuiers" (C, fol. 180). Charles le Conte was, as usual, heavily involved in all this work.

There remained the payment of personnel and labor. The King's archers and "canonniers" naturally took part; ammunition had to be provided, though the "lances à feu" originally intended for use were after all kept in store (C, fol. 185).[99] The biggest problem seems to have been the recruiting of crews to man the galleys. Over the following few days two sergents de ville were at the Porte de Charenton (on 5 June) and in various towns lining the river, on the lookout for able-bodied "gens de riuiere" and fishermen. The sergeants were relieved to have four copies of the letters royal "pour donner confort et ayder ceux commissaires depputez pour amener lesd. gens de riuiere" (C, fol. 195). Later, the "crieurs et trompette" received payment for making proclamations about the naval combat: forbidding the ferrying of unauthorized persons to the Ile aux Vaches where the galleys were stationed; forbidding unauthorized access to the Ile de Louviers; and forbidding the enrolled oarsmen to leave the town (C, fol. 202). And even when men were enlisted, some proved too old or otherwise unfit and had to be sent home; one individual turned out to have a criminal record and was taken into custody (C, fol. 188v). Then the recruiting of the "gens de guerre à pyé aduenturiers francoys" was delegated to Captain La Saulverie and the Vicomte de Beaupré (C, fol. 199). The first relevant entry mentions 400 men involved (ibid.); and the troops were apparently divided up as follows: La Saulverie had under his command 2 lieutenants, 2 standard-bearers, 1 "sergent de bataille," 6 "sergens de bande," 6 drummers, 2 fifes, the rest of the 160 men "picqueurs et harquebuziers" (ibid.). The Captain appears to have been paid 95 l.t. but the manuscript is slightly damaged at this point (C, fol. 200). The "monstre et veue" of this company took place on 3 July in Paris instead of at the port l'Archevesque, as had been previously arranged. Under the Vicomte de Beaupré there were 164 men, with 2 lieutenants, 2 standard-bearers, 6 "sergens de bende," 8 drummers, 4 fifes, the rest being "picqueurs et harquebuziers" (ibid.), and their parade occurred at the port l'Archevesque on the same day. Disbursements were made for feeding the men — 6 muys of claret and 1500 loaves of bread — and for a dinner enjoyed by the officers and N.C.O.s involved (C, fol. 201r-v). The overall bill came to 14, 171 l. 1 s. 11 d.t. (C, fol. 203).

One will have noticed the presence of a number of Italian craftsmen employed for the preparation of the naval combat; this may, as has been suggested, have been due to pressure from the Guise faction at court; at the same time, one would expect reliable and skilled technicians, already on the royal lists or of good standing in the light of their work at Fontainebleau, to be pressed into service anyhow. At all events, the entertainments were a great success.

> Le Mercredy suiuant, le Roy & la Royne prindrent apres leur soupper l'esbat d'une grande guerre nauale, entreprise par les Princes & Gentils-hommes de France, & par Messieurs de la Ville de Paris, pour la recreation de leurs Maiestez. Le Roy & la Royne par une braue Gondole furent menez dedans le bateau que la ville auoit faict dresser, & enrichir de leurs coulleurs: duquel ils virent descendre d'amont l'eaue trente trois galleres painctes de diuerses coulleurs, aux deuises des assaillans, & autrement bien garnies de forceres, & braues soldats: lesquelles de prinsault passantes à la file deuant le fort, basty au fons de l'Isle de Louuiers, le saluerent d'une espouentable infinité de cannonades, puis escarmouches de sept Galeaces, serrées dans le port, ioignant le fort, reculerent faisans semblant de fuyr, pour puis apres venir en foulle donner l'assault furieux: auquel d'entrée les tenans mirent le feu dedans l'une de leurs tours, fermant le haure: parce qu'ils ne la iugeoyent tenable & en dura la flamme une grand'heure pendant que les riues des Celestins, & Sainct Victor, couuertes de peuple dru comme sable, & d'un bouleuert de l'Isle aux Vaches, couuerte de soldats, doubles canons, couleurines, & harquebuzes à croc, estoyent la veuë & ouye aux spectateurs de ladicte fumée & tempeste qu'elles faisoyent. Les Galleres esparses sur l'eaue de tous les costez du fort, & les soldats Parisiens venans promptement au secours, partie dans autres batteaux & brigantins, assaillirent & eschellerent le fort, auec telles brauades: & furent repoulsez par les tenans, de pots & lances à feu, de coups de picques, d'espées, & haches, de telle constance & roydeur, que le Roy, les Dames, & les Seigneurs ne perdirent le plaisir de ce combat, iusques à dix heures du soir, que l'obscurité de la nuict contraignit les combatans & regardans de se departir, & retirer chacun chez soy, auec indicible liesse & contentement.[100]

The thunder of the artillery undoubtedly impressed the bystanders, as it had done during the Entry proper; and Corrozet, in his account, adds that

> de l'estonnement les verreries des Celestins tomberent toutes par terre, une gallerie fut bruslée par le feu qui se print à leur poudre estant ietté de ceux de dedans.[101]

Sauval remarks drily at a much later date that the

> depense au reste fut si grande que la Ville seule pour sa part déboursa soixante mille livres, & meme qu'il lui fallut emprunter.[102]

His figures seem to be well below those given by the *Comptes*; but, however one does the sums, the total disbursements made by the City for the Entry and the accompanying entertainments were exceptionally high.

(XIV) The Procession and Burning of Heretics on 4 July

The ceremonies of the Entry were still not ended, and the epilogue is played out on a more sombre note. Nevertheless, it is an essential part of the whole pageant, since it stresses the religious attitude that accompanies the assertion of royal power within and without the realm. Some contemporary accounts relate the events of 4 July fairly succinctly; a fuller report is provided, once again, by Belleforest:

> Le lendemain, qui fust le Ieudy quatriesme iour du mois de Iuillet dudict an, le Roy, meu de deuotion, & du tiltre de tres-Chrestien, affecté par prerogatiue à luy & tous ses predecesseurs Rois de France, fist une procession solennelle, afin qu'il pleust à Dieu extirper les heresies, & augmenter & asseurer la foy Chrestienne, qui de toute ancienneté a trouué soeur (*sic*) appuy, fondement & soubstentement en son Royaume. Pour laquelle celebrer partirent reueremment, & par son commandement de l'Eglise de S. Paul, les quatre ordres des Mendians de ladite Ville, precedes de toutes les bannieres des paroisses, & colleges, portans comme les Mendians chappes, & grand nombre de chasses, & reliquaires en grande reuerence & deuotion. Apres lesquels furent portees les chasses de Madame Sainte Geneviefue & Monsieur Sainct

Marceau, entourees & suiuies de citoyens nuds en chemises, auec les Religieux & abbé dudict conuent Saincte Geneviefue, aussi pieds nuds, portans tous un cierge de cire blanche en la main: au doz desquels se voyoit long ordre de ieunes Escoliers, & de tout le corps de l'Université de Paris, d'un costé des Ausmoniers & Chantres du Roy, & des Chanoines & dignitez de nostre Dame, & Saincte Chappelle de l'autre, portans aussi reueremment chascun un cierge de cire blanche en leur main: pressez des trompettes sonnantes, & des Suysses, marchans au son des Tabourins & Fiffres: & apres eux cent des Gentils-hommes de la maison du Roy, portans les Suysses une torche, garnie des armoiries de France, en la main droicte, la hallebarde en la gauche: les Gentilshommes, la hache d'armes d'une main, & de l'autre un gros flambeau ardent. Les abbez, Euesques & Archeuesques, qui les suiuoient, portoient tous en leurs mains des saincts & precieux reliquaires, tant du thresor de la Saincte chappelle, que d'ailleurs: & peu apres estoient portees reueremment les Sainctes reliques, sçauoir est la precieuse couronne d'espines, la Vraye Croix, les cloux, la Verge de Moyse, & autres sacrez reliquaires en grand nombre. Puis les Cardinaux deux à deux, vestus de leurs chappes de camelot violet, marchoient grauement deuant un riche ciel, couuert de broderie d'or, & de perles, portés par quatre Princes: soubs lequel Monsieur le Cardinal de Guyse portoit le Sainct Sacrement de l'autel: & estoit de pres suiuy par la maiesté du Roy, accompagné de monseigneur le reuerendissime Cardinal de Lorraine, de la Royne, & Dames de la Cour, toutes accostees des Princes, Seigneurs, & Gentilshommes, portans tout (*sic*) un cierge de cire blanche en la main. Apres eux venoient monsieur le Chancelier, & Maistre des Requestes de l'Hostel, la Cour de Parlement, en robbes rouges, Messieurs les Generaux des Aydes, & des Comptes: & les Preuosts & Escheuins, suiuis des notables Bourgeois & Marchans de la Ville, & fermez par derriere des Archers, portans tous chacun une torche, garnie des armoiries de France. En tel ordre & venerable deuotion passa la pompe solennelle iusques à la grande Eglise nostre Dame de Paris: où le Roy, & toute la cour, ouyt deuotement la Messe en grande solennité celebree: puis, ayant pris, auec la Royne, le disner au logis de l'Euesché, veid s'en retournant en sa maison des Tournelles, brusler vifs quelques Heretiques Sacramentaires, condamnez par sa cour de Parlement, à la rigueur des Ordonnances, que il & feu de bonne memoire le Roy François, son pere, ont faictes, pour l'extirpation & griefue punition de telles pernicieuses & damnables opinions.[103]

The procession went from Saint-Paul to Notre-Dame by way of the rue Saint-Antoine, the rue de la Tissanderie and the rue de la Coutellerie. Harangues to the King were made by the Cardinal de Guise, the Premier Président and the Prévôt des Marchands, representing the Church, the judiciary and the City respectively.

(xv) The Organization of the Entry: The Artists and Craftsmen Involved.

We have had occasion to mention various officials and artists or craftsmen involved as we discussed certain features of the Entry; but a clearer picture will emerge if we bring this information, with certain other details, together and try to assess as far as possible the part played by these various persons. In an organizational or consultative capacity, it is highly probable that Jean du Tillet, clerk to the Parlement, would offer the benefit of his experience. He had helped to lay down the ceremonial for the Entry of Eleanor of Austria; he had access to earlier Parlement records and had himself an impressive collection of information concerning previous Entries; and he was an authority on matters of precedence. But for the artistic aspects of the Entry other people would have to be brought into the picture — and here two points will strike one from the outset. In the first place, the Entry, in its organization and personnel, reflects in great measure the change in artistic direction that occurred on the accession of Henri II to the throne. He and Montmorency's faction were less sympathetic to the Italians, and the appointment of Philibert de l'Orme as supervisor of the royal buildings of 3 April 1548 marked the relative eclipse of Il Primaticcio, whose participation in the Entry is more or less restricted to areas where the Guises had some say. Nevertheless, two qualifications spring to mind: on the one hand, the City of Paris would be expected to draw on local talent as much as possible — there is an important economic and local side that must be taken into account; and at the same time, craftsmen of high quality, often employed by the King, would be hired for their skills, irrespective of other considerations. And on the other hand, one does note in the Entry the prolongation of artistic features associated with the previous reign: the recurrence of mythological motifs that had already served to embellish Fontainebleau — Vertumnus and Pomona, Flora, Hercules and Pan, *la France victorieuse* and *la France fertile*, not to speak of a triumph of Minerva and the presence of allegorical figures such as Prudence; and beneath the Pavillon du Portail, a vestibule contained among other things a representation of Hercules on the Argo.[104] In the second place, Henri II on his accession had in his neighborhood a number of artists in whom the ideals of neo-classicism and patriotism were well developed and who were obviously capable of working together; one of the striking features of the Entry is the sense of teamwork properly coordinated and organized.

This is where Jean Martin comes into the picture: as a man on good terms with various neo-classical artists, well versed in architectural matters and imbued with a strong cultural nationalism, he was well fitted to take a hand. The *Comptes* bring out his cardinal role:

> A Maistre Jehan Martin secretaire de Monseigneur le cardinal de Lenoncourt, La Somme de cent escuz soleil a xlv stz piece val. deux cens vingt cinq liures tournois . . . pour ses peines, sallaires et vaccations d'auoir inuenté, faict et conduict ses inuentions des arcs triumphans, obelisque et autres choses qui ont esté faictes pour lesdictes entrees. En quoy faisant il a vacqué continuelle-ment l'espace de cinq mois et plus pendant lequel temps il n'a sceu vacquer a ses affaires propres et en auroit discontinué son estude.
>
> (C, fol. 89 v)

He received payment for his duties on 31 July, so that the time scheme proves his involvement from the start. The terms suggest that he was responsible for the plans of the triumphal arches and, one would think, for the symbolism of the obelisk and other features on the arches. He had in some measure the services of Thomas Sebillet:

> A Maistre Thomas Sebillet, la Somme de vingt cinq escuz soleil payment was made on 17 August . . . pour le recompenser des peines, sallaires et vaccacions qu'il a faictz a la conduicte et inuen-tion des pictures faictes, tant ausditz arcs triumphans qu'en la salle de l'euesché de paris en laquelle a esté faict par ladicte ville le festin a la royne. Et ce auec ledict maistre Jehan Martin, dont ledict Sibillet n'auroit eu aulcun sallaire ne remuneration.
>
> (C, fol. 90)

Sebillet's role was a fairly modest one, given the payment he received; it is a pity the *pictures* are not more precisely defined. If paintings are meant literally, what then was his relation to the painters Dorigny and Cousin mentioned elsewhere in connection with the arches? or does *pic-ture* have the secondary Latin meaning of "picture in words," which

would confirm the view that he was responsible for the quatrains? We
have no corroborating evidence to show that there were inscriptions in
the "salle episcopale."

Though Philibert de l'Orme is not mentioned by name in the *Registres*
or *Comptes*, other sources prove his part in the Entry, which was hardly
surprising in view of his standing at Court: from 1548 to 1553 he was
taken up with the building of Anet and had been commissioned to ex-
ecute the tomb of Francis I at Saint-Denis. We have seen that he was
responsible for the stands used at the *sacre* of the Queen at Saint-Denis,
for the works in the parc des Tournelles, in so far as they were royal
commitments — including the "grande salle" — and the triumphal arch
opening onto the area of the tourney; and he appears to have had some
oversight of the erection of the "perspective." That is the measure of his
involvement that we can infer from the records.

Then we come to artists who often appear in the accounts as a trio —
Jehan Cousin, Charles Dorigny and Jehan Goujon. They were paid
3000 l.t. for their work on the triumphal arches, the fontaine du
Ponceau, the obelisk and the "perspective" (C, fol. 56 v); 300 l.t. for
replacing withered ivy and "bouys" on the Pont Notre-Dame and 303 l.
15 s.t. for damage caused through delay and the rains to the arches (C,
fol. 64 r–v); 500 l.t. for the decoration of the H-shaped arch (C, fol.
108v) and 750 l.t. for that of the "grant salle" in the bishop's palace (C,
fol. 125v–126r). Thus they take a prominent part in the proceedings:
Dorigny and Cousin are described as "painctres" and Jehan Goujon as
"tailleur de figures," "maistre tailleur" or "maistre ymagier." Because
they are so often grouped together, it is difficult to distinguish their individual contributions, though Goujon must have been responsible for
any sculpture work that was required. He received 45 l.t. for the
"figures" of the triumphal arches, the obelisk and the Pont Notre-
Dame, as well as other, unspecified features noted in the *livret* (C, fol.
89); Gébelin thought he might have fashioned the sculptures "en ronde
bosse," since this type of work fits in with his later activity.[105] Goujon's
most recent biographer confidently attributes to him the sculptures of
the fontaine du Ponceau,[106] and earlier historians of Paris have linked
his name with the fontaine des Innocents. It is reasonable to suppose
that he shared responsibility for other features, otherwise the *Comptes*
would hardly have lumped the three artists together so frequently.

Dorigny is in many ways the most elusive: his name appears from
time to time in the accounts for the building of Fontainebleau, and he
worked as early as 1535 on a monthly basis on the stucco of the "grande
galerie."[107] In 1535 there are several similar references to him in the

accounts where his name also appears as Dargny, and he turns up once more in the accounts for the years 1540–50. He was therefore a well-established artist; and though he usually figures in the *Comptes* with Cousin and Goujon, he alone is responsible for painting and decorating the fort on the Ile de Louviers. So far as Jehan Cousin's share is concerned, we have seen good reason for attributing to him a proper part in the creation of the "perspective"; and Maurice Roy has suggested that he may have helped to decorate the triumphal arch near the Tournelles.[108] Cousin had been employed on the 1540 Entry of the Emperor Charles V into Paris, so that his experience must have come in useful; and in a lawyer's minute of 2 December 1539, his name appears with those of Anthoine Félix and Pierre Préaux who are also hired for the 1549 Entry.[109]

The craftsman most heavily involved, however, was surely Charles le Conte, "maistre charpentier" of the City and "charpentier juré du roy"; here we shall briefly recapitulate the entries concerning him in the *Comptes*: (i) 2000 l.t. for the triumphal arches, the obelisk, the "perspective"—the contract of 3 March was settled on 24 August; (ii) 723 l.t. for work on the stands and "barrieres," including a bridge "traversant du boullevert pardessus le fossé et tenant à la planchette pour le passage de gens de cheual et de pié pendant que ladicte porte estoit fermée"; for erecting a large stand at Saint-Lazare, which was then reduced in height on the orders of Monsieur de Lezigny and provided with a "tribunal"; for 150 "toises de contrelisses" in the rue Saint-Antoine (C, fol. 74 ff.); (iii) 2900 l.t. for the very extensive works carried out in the episcopal palace (C, fol. 101 ff.); for the four stands erected in the rue Saint-Antione; and for the bridge and stairway "pour monter de l'eglise de Paris ou logis episcopal" (C, fol. 103v)—this contract was paid for also on 24 August; (iv) 750 l.t. for the carpentry on the H-shaped arch (C, fol. 105–06) and for the rebuilding of the Queen's stand, on the orders of the duc d'Aumale and others (C, fol, 106); (v) 300 l.t. for further modifications to the Queen's stand (C, fol. 107r -v); (vi) 26 l. 10 s.t. for a partition in the "grande salle" of the Bishop's palace and for a buffet on which to place the silver present to the Queen (C, fol. 123v–124); (vii) for work connected with the naval combat: 191 l. 1 s.t.; Le Conte also provided cranes and built a bridge on the Ile de Louviers ("servant au bastion de la royne"), and prepared the model according to which the galleys were to be constructed (C, 170v and 172); (viii) 650 l.t. for preparing the latrines on the Ile de Louviers (C, fol. 180v). There was also a contract for delivering wood for 750 l.t. but a rebate was allowed for if Le Conte could reclaim some of the prime materials (C, fol. 181); (ix) 750 l.t. for building "une salle et gallerie construicte sur un grand basteau" for the King and Queen attending the naval combat (C, fol. 182v). By definition Charles le Conte was a key figure in the arrangements.

The *Comptes* also mention a host of craftsmen whose services were recruited: some, like Antoine Morisseau, master locksmith, or Nicolas Potier, master mason, or Guillaume de Saint-Jorre, paver, play important roles, and like Scibec, turn up in the accounts of royal buildings under construction before or after the Entry. Minor tasks were turned over to painters such as Antoine Félix, Pierre de Granville and Jehan Patin (C, fol. 64v, 71r–v, 71v, respectively); and the names of Jacques Conte and Martin Frelon are also to be found (C, fol. 108). The number of skilled craftsmen involved was thus impressive, and further disbursements were made to unskilled labor, tradesmen who furnished raw materials, as well as to victuallers.

D. Conclusion

The generous records we possess offer a wide-ranging and exciting picture of this Entry, which was outstanding in its *splendeurs* and its *misères*: at one end of the scale we see the petty wranglings on matters of precedence, the infighting that seems to have gone on between factions at Court, the mutterings of the Paris crowd, the reluctance of fishermen and "gens de riviere" to be frogmarched from their lucrative ploys to service in the galleys; at the other end, an exhibition of pageantry that rightly provoked admiration, indeed astonishment, from contemporaries. To the birth of this Entry there contributed factors and pressures of great variety: the soured relations between King and City, the growing ambitions of bodies in the realm that will gradually become more and more instruments of central power, threats from strong enemies outside the country and from religious dissidence within, cultural rivalry from a city like Lyon, financial problems, and perhaps other elements. The Entry is of course among other things a massive affirmation of force and national pride, a warning to foreign foe and internal dissenters alike. It is also a sign that royal authority is being gradually consolidated: the presentation of the King seems to be on a greater scale than was the case even in earlier Entries. By its stress on dynastic symbolism and the King as a unifying force, it foreshadows the time when the King is deemed to rule by Divine Right and enjoy absolute power. The fact that such detailed records were kept of this Entry also points in this direction. Nor is it without significance that more than any previous Entry, 1549 shows a shift from popular participation to a royal spectacle. In this context, the neo-classical principles that underlie the Entry, serve only to enhance the stature and dignity of the King; even the strong dose of erudition, while giving expression to an exalted view of national culture, helps to insert a wedge between the King and the plebs, unable to grasp all the symbolism of such a grandiose pageant. The aesthetic of the Entry helps to set the seal on a new conception of architectural design; it ushers in a new period of cultural splendor and expresses ideals that form part of the High Renaissance in sixteenth-century France.

Notes

1. Corrozet, fol. 168r.
2. G. Paradin, 655–56.
3. The state funeral of Francis I took place 22 May, 1547. See work by Ralph E. Giesey mentioned in the Bibliography.
4. See Bibliography.
5. See Bryant, 76.
6. G. Paradin, 651.
7. See below, section viii.
8. There seems to be a discrepancy here, since Le Conte had already entered a contract with the City in respect of this last matter on 3 March.
9. According to Belleforest, fol. 575v, proclamation was made on 8 April and 15 May.
10. R, 162–63; Godefroy, 1, 1007 ff.; Félibien, 5 (*Preuves* 3), 360 ff. The *Comptes*, fol. 81, state that the Dauphin stayed at the "logis de monsieur de Maigny."
11. The *Comptes*, fol. 64r–v, mention disbursements to craftsmen and artists for making good damage done to the decorations by the weather.
12. Crévier, 5, 443; see also Bulaeus, 6, 429 ff. for a fuller account.
13. Vieilleville's estimates suggest that in the King's cortège there were something like 2000 pages and a similar number of courtiers (*Mémoires*, 303). But he is not always accurate.
14. See Bryant, 163 ff.
15. Details are omitted from the *livret*, but have been preserved in the *Registres capitulaires* (AN LL 248, pp. 692, 694, 696–700, 702–06, 710–11).
16. Maurice Roy, "La collaboration de Philibert de l'Orme aux préparatifs de l'Entrée de Henri II à Paris et du sacre de Catherine de Médicis en 1549," *Revue du seizième siècle* 5 (1917–18): 209–223.
17. Belleforest, 576.
18. See also Corrozet, fol. 169v–170.
19. Andrea Fulvio, *Opera . . . della antichità della Città de Roma*, Venice, 1543, fol. 172v.
20. M-R. Jung, *Hercule dans la littérature française du XVIe siècle*, Geneva, 1966.
21. Cl. Paradin, 30.
22. See observations by Simon Renard (Imperial ambassador) in his despatch quoted by Anne Denieul-Cormier in *The Renaissance in France*, translated by A. and C. Fremantle, London, 1969, p. 249. The despatch was first reproduced in the *Bulletin de la Société de l'Histoire de France*, 1878.

23. Stewart, 4.

24. Ibid.,13.

25. Cl. Paradin, 112-13.

26. Bryant, 338-39.

27. V. Cartari, *Les Images des dieux des anciens* . . . (translated by A. du Verdier), 1606, p. 712. The work originally appeared in 1556.

28. "Prosphonematique au Roy Treschrestien Henry II," *Oeuvres poétiques,* ed. H. Chamard (STFM), 3, 61-74.

29. Tervarent, 171.

30. Bryant, 324, who refers to Dora and Erwin Panofsky, *Pandora's Box: the changing Aspects of a mythical Symbol,* New York, 1956.

31. Cartari, *Les Images des dieux,* 678.

32. L. Lalanne, *The Book of Fortune.* Two hundred unpublished Drawings by Jean Cousin, translated by H. Mainwaring Dunstan, Paris & London, 1883, Drawing cxiii, "Eloquentiae comes bona Fortuna."

33. *Andreae Alciati Emblematum libri duo,* Lyon, Jean de Tournes & G. Gazier, 1547, p. 20.

34. Cl. Paradin, 161.

35. Stewart, 12.

36. See works in Bibliography by Asher, Dubois and Simone.

37. Stewart, 11.

38. See Margaret McGowan, "Forms and themes in Henri II's entry into Rouen," *Renaissance drama* 1 (1968): 199-251.

39. Sometimes the *Registres* go further than the *livret* in this respect. It is probable that Jean Martin was responsible for both texts, at any rate up to a point.

40. P. du Colombier, *Jean Goujon,* 1949, 56-57.

41. See section xv.

42. *L'Architecture de Philibert de l'Orme* . . . , 1576, in particular the Preface, fol. 6 ff.

43. G. du Choul, *Discours de la Religion des anciens Romains,* Lyon, G. Rouille, 1556, pp. 36-37.

44. *Architecture ou Art de bien bastir de Marc Vitruve Pollion Autheur Romain antique* . . . (Martin's translation), 1547, fol. D iiij r (second series).

45. S. Serlio, *Il primo libro d'architectura* . . . , 1545 (Book 4), fol. xiv.

46. Ibid., fol. xxv v.

47. Ibid., fol. xvi v.

48. Ibid., fol. xvi.

49. Anthony Blunt, *Art and Architecture in France 1500-1700,* 1953, pp. 19-20. Francis I had a statue of Hercules by Michelangelo, who at one time thought of fleeing to France.

50. P. du Colombier, *Jean Goujon,* 10.

51. Bryant, 233.

52. S. Serlio, *Il primo libro,* Book 4, fol. xlvii v.

53. Bryant, 255. E. Coyecque, *Recueil d'actes notariés relatifs à l'histoire de Paris et de ses environs,* 1905-, vol. 2, 327-28, Item 5221, has the following entry:

François Chambéry, joueur de phifre . . . Philippe Chasteau, savetier, aussi joueur de tabourin . . . avecques une tierce personne, jouant duement du tabourin . . .

They played for two whole days, one for the King's Entry, one for the Queen's, as had been promised to one Chandrieu. The musicians were dressed in "drap noir" and a "bonnet noir," with the cost specified, but it is not clear where they were stationed to perform their duties.

54. Bryant, 293.

55. Serlio, *Il primo libro*, Book 4, fol. lxii v.

56. Corrozet, fol. 171.

57. P. du Colombier, *Jean Goujon*, 56–57.

58. Ibid., 54.

59. Maurice Roy, *Artistes et monuments de la Renaissance en France*, 1 (1929), 57.

60. See Bryant, 313, and D. and E. Panofsky, *Pandora's Box: the changing Aspects of a mythical Symbol*, London and New York, 1956.

61. *Liure de Perspectiue de Iehan Cousin*, Paris, Iehan le Royer, 1560, fol. C iv v.

62. Serlio, *Il primo libro*, 4, lxiii v.

63. On the Diana myth, see Françoise Bardon, *Diane de Poitiers et le mythe de Diane*, 1963.

64. Corrozet, fol. 169v.

65. Maurice Roy, *Artistes et monuments*, 200. He quotes from the minutes of G. Payen; but he does not give the manuscript source, and the details contained therein could refer to an additional "grant salle."

66. *L'Architecture*, fol. 218v.

67. Bryant, 28.

68. Cl. Paradin, 20. On all this, see Tervarent, 254. The sense of "orbem" is ambiguous.

69. F. Gébelin, "Un manifeste de l'Ecole classique en 1549: L'Entrée de Henri II à Paris," *Bulletin de la Société d'Histoire de Paris*, 51 (1924): 44, n. 1.

70. P. Giovio & G. Symeoni, *Dialogo dell'Imprese militari et amorosi*, Lyon, 1574, p. 57.

71. A. Alciat, *Emblematum libri duo*, J. de Tournes & G. Gazeau, Lyon, 1547. I use the edition nearest in date to the Entry. On emblems see A. Henkel & A. Schöne, *Emblematik. Handbuch zur Sinnbildkunst des XVI. und XVII. Jahrhunderts*, Stuttgart, 1967.

72. *L'Architecture de bien bastir du Seigneur Leon Baptiste Albert . . .* 1553, fol. 166.

73. *La magnificence de la superbe entree de la cité de Lyon faicte au roy Henry deuxiesme*, Lyon, 1549, fol. D 3.

74. It is not mentioned in either Tervarent or in Henkel & Schöne, though the latter do list the case of a sword inserted in a book (but without transfixing it): the meaning given is the victory of Learning over War. G. Symeoni,

Imprese . . . , 1561, p. 18, mentions the emblem *Ex utroque Caesar,* in which the ruler holds a sword in his right hand and a book in his left.

75. Tervarent, 64.

76. Ibid., 50.

77. *Le Songe de Poliphile,* fol. c.

78. Tervarent, 277.

79. In the 1553 edition of Martin's translation, fol. 110v-111.

80. Cf. *Aeneid,* 1. 78: "Tu mihi quodcumque hoc regni, tu sceptra Iouemque/Concilias"; though perhaps Ovid, *Fasti,* 1, 337, is also in play.

81. *Livret,* fol. 10. The *Registres,* 175 have ἀλεξιχλεως, a word not attested in Liddell and Scott.

82. The case for Sebillet is made out by V.-L. Saulnier, "L'Entrée de Henri II à Paris et la révolution poétique de 1550," *Les Fêtes de la Renaissance,* ed. J. Jacquot, 1956, pp. 31-59.

83. V.-L Saulnier, "L'Entrée." The term "Pléiade's" is a term of convenience to designate the group of poets clustering round Ronsard and Du Bellay in the middle 1550s.

84. "A Jan Martin," *Oeuvres complètes,* ed. P. Laumonier (STFM), 1, 131-35.

85. Joachim du Bellay, *Oeuvres poétiques,* ed. H. Chamard 1, vii (*Avertissement*).

86. Pierre de Ronsard, *Oeuvres complètes,* ed. P. Laumonier (STFM), 1, 17-23.

87. *Salmonij Macrini Iuliodunensis Cubicularij Regij Epitome Vitae Domini nostri Iesu Christi, ad Margaritam Valesiam Henrici Francorum Regis sororem unicam. varia item poematia, et de sacra Regis unctione, & de eiusdem triumphali in urbem Lutetiam introitu.* Paris, M. David, 1548 (Copies BN, OB). The three poems in question are: "De Henrici Secundi Gallorum Regis Christianiss. vnctione" (pp. 18-19); "Ad Catherinam Reginam Franciae Christianiss." (pp. 20-21); "De Regis et reginarum ingressu in urbem Lutetiam" (pp. 23-25). This last poem is reproduced below in the Appendix.

88. Belleforest, fol. 575v. The tourney was proclaimed also in Italy, Germany and Spain, according to Saulx-Tavannes, *Mémoires,* 127.

89. H. Sauval, *Histoire et recherches des Antiquités de la Ville de Paris,* 1724, 2, 692.

90. The *Registres,* 162, under 3 May, record that an inspection of various sites took place with Charles le Conte; and it was decided, among other things, to "faire le parron à Saint Ladre" and, owing to Henri II's pressing interest, to "aller en dilligence despauer la rue Sainct Anthoine à l'endroit où il convient faire lesd. lisses."

91. Information about the craftsmen and minor artists employed for the Entry is sometimes scanty; the most useful sources are: L. de Laborde, *La Renaissance des arts à la cour de France,* 1886; also his *Les Comptes des bâtiments du roi (1528-1571);* U. Thieme, F. Becker and collaborators, *Allgemeines Lexikon der bildenden Künstler,* 36 vols. Leipzig, 1907-47.

92. L. Dimier, *Le Primatice peintre, sculpteur et architecte des rois de France,* 1900, p. 175.

93. Belleforest, fol. 576. See also Saulx-Tavannes, *Mémoires,* 127.

94. Belleforest, fol. 576v.

95. *Copia d'una lettera . . . sopra la Festa fatta in Roma, nella piazza di Santo Apostolo, per il nascimento del Duca d'Orleans . . . ,* n.p.,n.d., fol. A v. There is a copy of this rare text in the BL, though the French translation is fairly well known. The best known account is naturally Rabelais' *Sciomachie.*

96. M. Roy, *Artistes et monuments,* 295; *Allgemeines Lexikon . . . ,* 30, 578.

97. Minutes of J.T. in M. Roy, *Artistes et monuments,* 186.

98. Ibid., 436–43. On L. Penni see *Allgemeines Lexikon . . . ,* 26, 348.

99. Belleforest's account, given below, takes a different view.

100. Belleforest, fol. 576r–v.

101. Corrozet, fol. 170.

102. H. Sauval, *Histoire et Recherches,* 2, 678.

103. Belleforest, fol. 576v–577. The *Registres,* 184, also give details. Félibien, 4 (*Preuves* 2), 745, publishes the account from the *Registres* of the Parlement de Paris (AN X^{IA} 1565, fol. 214v). See also AN LL 215 (formerly 248), which contains the minutes of the Chapter of Notre-Dame. The *Registres,* 185, reproduce the substance of the Prévôt's speech.

104. L. Dimier, *Le Primatice,* 77 and 295–99.

105. F. Gébelin, "Un Manifeste," 43.

106. P. du Colombier, *Jean Goujon,* 69.

107. M. Roy, *Artistes et monuments,* 234. See also *Allgemeines Lexikon . . .* 9, 474.

108. M. Roy, *Artistes et monuments,* 68.

109. On A. Félix, see *Allgemeines Lexikon . . . ,* XI, 371.

Appendix

Jean Salmon Macrin:
"De Regis et reginarum ingressu in urbem Lutetiam"
(see above, note 87)

Parhisiam cum Rex intrauit Gallicus urbem,
    Inque cataphracto sedit honorus equo:
Vicit Alexandri festos ea pompa triumphos,
    Romulei egerunt quosque aliquando Duces.
Anteibant proceres auro fulgentibus armis
    Lecti omnes, equitum pone magister erat.
Inde sub umbella, argento gemmisque decorus
    Maiestate suos Rex specieque premit.
Auricomus Titan ut caetera praeterit astra,
    Et phoenix alias Indicus inter aues.
Regius a tergo sequitur pulchro ordine sanguis,
    In quo Vindocinus primus honore fuit.
Mox reliqui sacra prognati ab origine Regum,
    Torquibus, auratis conspicuique sagis.
Ast alacri plebes viuat Rex intonat ore,
    Ingressoque urbem prospera fata rogat.
Hac summam serie Rex tandem incessit ad aedem,
    Ante Deum flexo procubuitque genu.
Cuius adorauit syncero pectore numen,
    Exposcens sophiam qua data regna regat.
Auspiciis Salomon primis ita cernuus olim,
    Talia ab aetherea dona poposcit ope.
Vrbem at enim postquam Regina intrauit eandem,
    (Lux ea ab ingressu tertia Regis erat)
Nulla aeque flexere oculos spectacula nostros,
    Atque magis grata detinuere mora:
Quam quae & Reginam & Regis lectica sororem
    Aduerso positas vexit aperta loco.
Nec mirabamur baccata monilia, gemmas,

Picta nec auratis serica textilibus.
Nec quam gestabant proceres praediuitis urbis
    Umbellam pulchris conspicui in togulis.
Regali neque matronas a sanguine claras,
    Ex auro pressit queis diadema caput.
Sed Reginarum iubar immortale duarum,
    Quas currus niueis ipse vehebat equis.
Sed consensum animi, sancti sed foedus amoris,
    Qui nodo Herculeo firmus utranque ligat.
Altera Lucinae quater ante experta laborem,
    Eximia Francas prole beauit opes.
Altera virginei illibato flore pudoris,
    Expectat digni laetitiam thalami.
O felix lectica, sacram quam dicere mensam
    Non dubitem, geminas cum ferat ipsa Deas?
Hanc ego vbi pompam conspexi, defluus imber
    Laetitiae ex oculis signa fuere meae.
Elicuere mihi lachrymas nam gaudia largas,
    Spectarem te illo quod residere gradu,
Vnica magnanimi Francisci o nata superstes.
    Nec potui patris non meminisse tui,
Fratris & Henrici qui tunc, pulcherrima Nympha,
    Ostendit liquido quam sibi chara fores:
Te quia honorata iungi cum compare iussit,
    Gloria tantum non par ut, & aequa foret.
Et cur diuideret, quas sic concordia nectit,
    Vt non esse duas velle recludat idem?
Nimirum haec adeo populus spectacula probauit,
    Maius ut in pompa duxerit esse nihil.
Mactae ambae virtute pares, saluo illa fruatur,
    At tandem digno Nympha iugere viro.
Deinde & percipias fructus quos illa, feratur
    Nupta diu, Franci tu Iouis esse soror.

Bibliography

Books published after 1600 in French and English appear at Paris and London respectively, unless otherwise indicated. Some titles of books published before that date are given in slightly abbreviated form.

I EVENTS LEADING UP TO THE ENTRY AND FEATURING IN CONTEMPORARY DOCUMENTS

a. Charles V's Entry into Paris 1540

La sontuosa intrata di Carolo, sempre Augusto in la Grā Citta di Parigi, con gli apparati, triūphi, feste, archi triomphali, liuree, presenti, cirimonie Ecclesiastice, & pope Regale, fatte a sua. in Francia, n.p., n.d. (the text is dated Paris, 3 January 1540). 4°.　　　　　　　　　　　BL

El grāde y muy sumptuoso recibimiento que hizieron en la gran cibdad de Paris: al Inuictissimo Emperador y rey nuestro señor. n.p., n.d. 4°.　　BL

Lordre tenu et garde a Lentree de treshault & trespuissant prince Charles . . . , Paris, G. Corrozet & Jehan du Pré, 1539. 8°.　　　　　　BN

La Magnificque et Triumphante Entrée de tres illustre et sacré Empereur Charles . . . , Lyon, F. Juste, n.d. 4°.　　　　　　　　　　　BN

b. The King at Rheims in 1547

Le Sacre et Couronnement du Roy Henry deuxieme de ce nom. (Paris), R. Estienne, n.d. 8°.　　　　　　　　　BL, BN, OB, TC Dublin

La Intrata del re christianissimo Henrico nella citta di Rens e la sua incoronatione. Vinegia, 1547. 8°.　　　　　　　　　　　　　　FW

Jacobus Chichon, *De adeptione Regni, consecratione, & coronatione Henrici Secundi, Francorum Regis, inuictissimi, deque ingressu illius in ciuitate Rhemensi Ecphrasis,* Paris, Matthieu David, 1547. 4°BL,BN

Franciscus & Claudius fratres Lestrangii, *Orationes duae de regia consecratione, a duobus nobilissimis adolescentibus . . . habitae in gymnasio Praeleorum,* Paris, Matthieu David, 1547. 8°.   BL, BN

F. Godefroy, *Ceremonial de France . . .* 1, 303–09: *La reception du mesme Roy Henry dans la ville de Rheims, lorsqu'il y arriua pour son sacre. . .*

c. Entry into Lyon 1548

Le grand Triumphe faict à l'entrée du Treschrestien et tousiours victorieux Monarche, Henry second de ce nom Roy de France, en sa noble ville et cité de Lyon, Et de la Royne Catherine son espouse . . . , Paris, B. de Gourmont, 1548. 8°. BN

Another issue n.p.1548.4°.   BN

La magnificence de la superbe et triumphante entree de la cité noble et antique faicte au Treschrestien Roy de France Henry deuxiesme de ce nom . . . , Lyon, G. Rouille, 1549. 4°.   BL, OB

La magnifica et triumphale entrata del re di Francia Henrico secondo . . . fatta nella . . . Città di Lyone . . . Lyon, G. Rouille, 1549. 4°.   BL,OB

d. Celebrations in Rome of the Birth of Louis duc d'Orléans

Copia d'una lettera scritta all'Illustriss. et Reuerendiss. Cardinal di Ferrara, sopra la Festa fatta in Roma, nella piazza di Santo Apostolo, per il nascimento del Duca d'Orléans . . . n.p., n.d. (Signed A.B.) 4°.   BL

La magnificence des triumphes faictz à Rome, pour la natiuité de Monseigneur le Duc d'Orleáns second filz du Roy Treschrestien Henry deuxiesme de ce nom. Traduicte d'Italien en Francoys. Paris, J. André & G. Corrozet, 1549. 4°.   BN

Another issue by the same printers, 1549. 8°.   BN

F. Rabelais, *La Sciomachie et festins faictz a Rome au palais de M. reuerendissime Cardinal du Bellay, pour l'heureuse naissance de Monseigneur d'Orleans,* Lyon, S. Gryphe, 1549. 8°.   BN

II Preliminary announcements; publications concerning related events

a. *Publication du iour de l'Entrée du roy treschrestien Henry deuxiesme de ce nom en la ville de Paris,* J. André & G. Corrozet, 1549. 8°.   BN

b. *L'Ordre et les articles du Tournoy entrepris pour la solennité du tresheureux couronnement et triumphante entrée du treschrestien Roy Henry . . . et de la Royne son espouse . . . enuoyez de par sa maiesté à Messeigneurs de la Court de Parlement de Paris et publiez par les Heraux de France, sur la pierre de Marbre du Palais dudict lieu, le premier iour du mois d'auril 1548.* Paris, P. & J. Roffet, n.d. 4°.   BN

Another issue, P. & J. Roffet, n.d. 8°.   BN

Another issue, Paris, J. André, 1548 (n.s. 1549). 8°.   BN

Another edition, Lyon, J. Gillet, 1549. 8°.   BN

c. Entry of Dauphin: in F. Godefroy, 1, 1007 ff.

d. *Sacre* of the Queen

C'est l'ordre et forme qui a esté tenu au Sacre & Couronnement de treshaulte & tresillustre Dame Catherine de Medicis, Royne de France, faicte en l'Eglise Monseigneur sainct Denys en France, le X. iour de Iuin. M.D.XLIX., Paris, J. Dallier, n.d. 4°.   BL, BN, OB

Another issue, Paris, J. Dallier, n.d. 4°.   BL, BN, Toulouse

Another issue, Paris, J. Roffet, n.d. 4°.   BN, NLS

e. *Articles contenans les causes qui ont meu le Roy nostre Seigneur Henry deuxiesme de ce nom, treschrestien à faire la procession generale à Paris, ville capitale de son royaume, le quatriesme iour de iuillet 1549.* Paris, Andry Roffet, dict le Faulcheur, n.d. (mentioned in M. Roy, op. cit., 212)   BN Rothschild

III THE *livret* OF THE ENTRY

A. C'est l'ordre qui a este te- | NV A LA NOVVELLE ET
IOYEVSE | entrée que treshault, tresexcellẽt, & trespuissãt
Prince, | le Roy treschrestien Henry deuzieme de ce nom, à fai- |
ete en sa bonne ville & cité de Paris, capitale de son Royaume, le
sezieme iour de Iuin M.D.XLIX. | [The large device of Jacques
Roffet in surround with "faulcheur" facing left] | On les vend à
Paris chez Iacques Roffet dict le Faul- | cheur, en la rue Geruais
Laurẽs, à l'enseigne du souf- | flet pres Saincte Croix en la cité. |
PAR PRIVILEGE DV ROY.

38 ff. a–g iv + A iv, B vi. 4°.

The two illustrations of the Arch in front of the Palais de Justice
and the final Triumphal Arch (on a *dépliant*) are separate.
    1v Privilege granted for one year to Jacques Roffet, dated
Chantilly 31 March 1548 (a.s. 1549)
    2 C'est l'ordre qui a esté te- | NV A LA NOVVELLE ET
IOYEV- | se entrée . . .
    29 Sensuit l'ordre de lentree | DE LA ROYNE
    38v End of text   BL, BN, CUL

B. C'est l'ordre qui a este te- | NV A LA NOVVELLE ET
IOYEVSE | entrée, que treshault, tresexcellent, & trespuissant |
Prince la Roy treschrestien Henry deuzieme | de ce nom, á faicte
en sa bonne ville et ci- | té de Paris, capitale de son Royaume, | le
sezieme iour de Iuin | M.D.XLIX. [Roffet's device, but smaller
than in A] | On les vend á Paris par Jehan Dallier sur le pont
sainct Michel à l'enseigne de la Rose blanche. | PAR
PRIVILEGE DV ROY.
Apart from the title page, the issue appears to be similar to **A.** BN

C. C'est l'ordre qui a este te- | NV A LA NOVVELLE ET
IOYEVSE | entrée, que treshault, tresexcellent, & trespuissant |
Prince le Roy treschrestien Henry deuzieme | de ce nom, à faicte
en sa bonne ville & ci- | té de Paris, capitale de son Royaume, | le
sezieme iour de Iuin | M.D.XLIX. | [Printer's device of man hoe-
ing near tree in oblong frame — Roffet's device] | On les vend à
Paris par Iehan Dallier sus le pont Sainct | Michel à l'enseigne de
la Rose blanche.

41 ff. + 2 unnumbered ff. a–g iv + A–D iv. 4°.

The two illustrations of the Arch in front of the Palais de Justice and the final Triumphal Arch (on a *dépliant*) are separate as before. The text differs substantially, after fol. 35, from other issues, with a long new section from 35v to 38v, describing the dinner and the present offered to the Queen and the present for the King. After fol. 37 the sheets are incorrectly numbered (37, 40, 39, 38, 37). On fol. 40 (= 38), the Prévôt des Marchand's request that the King follow tradition in agreeing to come on the following Sunday to the place de Grève in celebration of St John the Baptist is reported, as is his presence on the day stated. This is therefore a different edition, and as it gives the fullest text of the *livret*, is reproduced here.   BN, Toulouse

D. C'EST L'ORDRE QVI | A ESTE TENV A LA NOVVELLE | ET IOYEVSE ENTREE, QVE TRES- | hault, tresexcellent, & trespuissant Prince, le Roy | treschrestien Henry deuxiesme de ce nom, a faicte en sa bonne ville & cité de Paris, | capitale de son Royaume, le se- | ziesme iour de Iuing | M.D.XLIX | Device (fleuron) | A PARIS, | Par Iean Dallier Libraire, demourant sur le pont sainct | Michel à l'enseigne de la Rose blanche. | PAR PRIVILEGE DV ROY.

38 ff. a–g iv + A iv, B iv, 4°.

The type is new, and there are different conventions for spelling and abbreviations. The *privilège* is not reproduced on fol. 1v.   BN, OB

The Bibliothèque Municipale, Toulouse has a copy (Rés. C XVI 78) with the title page missing; it appears to be either **A** or **B**. The copy in the NLS (Newbattle 3737[1]) is not yet accessible to the public, but is, so far as the short-title description allows one to judge either **B** or **C**. Another copy, not seen by myself, is in Harvard College Library: see *Harvard College Library, French XVIth-century Books,* vol. 1, Item 202 (pp. 246–48), where a reference is made to Fairfax Murray, 1, 150). It is an **A** copy.

IV OTHER CONTEMPORARY PUBLICATIONS DESCRIBING OR CELEBRATING THE ENTRY

These do not carry the authority of Jean Martin's text, but are valuable for further details they supply, though each text varies in its emphasis:

e. g. the *Grands triumphes* published at Paris pay much attention to the order of the procession, whereas John Stewart is offering us a more formal, humanist harangue.

Les grands triumphes faictz a lentree du treschrestien & victorieux Roy Henry second de ce nom, En sa noble ville cité & université de Paris. Paris, Germain de la Fosse, n.d. 8°.   BL, BN

Les Grandes Triumphes faictes a l'entrée du treschrestien et victorieux roy Henry, second de ce nom, en sa noble ville, cité et Vniuersité de Paris. Rouen, Le Prestre, n.d. 8°.   BN

Entrée de Henri II à Paris. n.p., n.d. 8°.   BN

Ferrand de Bez, *Le Grand Triumphe magnificque des Parisiens, de la venue du treschrestien roy Henry second de ce nom, En sa Ville de Paris . . . Auec une epistre a la royne.* Paris, Nicolas Buffet, n.d. 8°.   BN

John Stewart, *De aduentu Henrici Valesii Christianissimi Francorum Regis in Metropolim Regni Sui Lutetiam Parisiorum oratio habita . . . in gymnasio Prelleorum.* Paris, Matthieu David, 1549. 4°.
                                                                    BL, BN,NLS

Joachim du Bellay, *Prosphone(u)matique au Roy Treschrestien Henry II.* Paris, G. Cavellat, 1549. 8°.   BN
The title page of the BN copy is now missing, but is described by Marty-Laveaux and also in the B.N. *Catalogue de l'Histoire de France,* 1, 241. The poem was reprinted in the *Recueil de Poesie,* November 1549, and is reproduced in the Chamard edition of the *Oeuvres poétiques* (STFM), 3, 61–74.

P. de Ronsard, *Avantentrée du Roy Treschrestien à Paris.*
 According to P. Laumonier in his edition of the *Oeuvres complètes* (STFM), 1, vii, the first edition published by G. Corrozet, 1549, 4°, is now unknown, but there was a second edition, and the poem was reprinted in the *Bocage* of 1550; it is reproduced in the STFM edition, 1, 17–23.

Jean Salmon Macrin, "De Regis et reginarum ingressu in urbem Lutetiam," *Epitome Vitae Domini nostri Iesu Christi . . . varia item poematia, & de sacra Regis unctione, & de eiusdem triumphali in urbem*

Lutetiam introitu. Paris, Matthieu David, 1549. 8°.   BN, OB

V Contemporary manuscript sources

P. Guérin,   *Registre des délibérations du bureau de la ville de Paris,* III, 1886.

AN   KK 286 A, The indispensable accounts of the Entry, recorded by Philippe Macé on fol. 53–203.

AN   X^{IA} 1565. Registers of the Council of the Parlement de Paris (fol. 172–74).

AN   LL 145 (formerly 248). Chapter of Notre-Dame: minutes of the reception at Notre-Dame (pp. 703–12).

AN   KK 286. *Registres des Comptes de la Maison du Roi.*

BN   Dupuy 325. Account by Jean du Tillet (pp. 79–98).

BN   ms fçs 20613 (pp. 597–605). *C'est l'ordre qui a esté tenu à l'entrée solemnelle de Henry 2 Treschrestien Roy de France en sa capitale Ville de Paris le (x)vi iour de Iuin mil^{vc} xlix.*

BN   Estampes 1d. 18 Cérémonies et entrées triomphales de 1500 à 1640.

Some information may also be gleaned from AN K 957 and from BN fonds Fontanieu, nouv. acq. fçses, no. 7644; also from notarial records published in M. Roy, *Artistes et monuments de la Renaissance en France.* Simon Renard's despatch, published originally in the *Bulletin de la Société de l'Histoire de Paris,* 1878, has been quoted recently in Anne Denieul-Cormier, *The Renaissance in France,* trans. A. and C. Fremantle, 1969, p. 249.

VI Records published by earlier historians

F. Godefroy, *Cérémonial de France,* 1641, 2 vols. The relevant material is in Vol. 1.

(i) *Sacre* at Rheims, 26 July 1547	1,279 ff.
(ii) Entry into Rheims	1,330 ff.
(iii) *Sacre* and coronation of the Queen	1,510–18
(iv) Transcript of the *livret* of the Entry	1,858–69
(v) *Procez verbal de ladicte entrée* . . . by Jean du Tillet, Greffier du Parlement	1,879–85
(vi) *Le Rang du Chancelier à l'entrée du Roy*	1,885–86

(vii) Jean du Tillet's account of the Queen's Entry   1, 887–93
(viii) Entry of the Dauphin (11 June), from the *Registres de la Ville*
                                                            1, 1007 ff.

P. Félibien, *Histoire de la Ville de Paris,* éd. revue et augmentée par D. Guy-Alexis Lobineau, 5 vols. 1725. The relevant volume is 5 (*Preuves* 3).

(i) Entry of Henri II (*Registres de la Ville*)   5, 361–74
(ii) Entry of the Queen   5, 374 ff.
(iii) Entry of the Dauphin   5, 360–61
(iv) The fort on the Ile de Louviers   5, 381

Further details may be obtained from the following:

> Bulaeus (C. Egasse du Boulay). *Historia Universitatis parisiensis,* 6 vols. 1665–73. See in particular 6, 429–32.
> Coyecque, E. *Recueil d'actes notariés relatifs à l'histoire de Paris et de ses environs,* 1905–, vol. 2, 327–28.
> Crévier, J. B. L. *Histoire de l'Université de Paris depuis son origine jusqu'en l'année 1600,* 7 vols., 1761. See especially 5, 439–45.
> Du Tillet, Jean. *Recueil des Rangs des Grands de France,* 1601. See especially pp. 99–100 (The King's dinner on 16 June) and pp. 100–1 (2 July 1549). See also under Godefroy.
> Sauval, Henri. *Histoire et recherches des Antiquitez de Paris,* 1724, vol. 2, 639 ff. (on Royal Entries generally).

VII ACCOUNTS BY CONTEMPORARY HISTORIANS AND WRITERS OF MEMOIRS

> Belleforest, F. de in Nicolas Gilles, Denys Sauvage, F. de Belleforest, G. Chappuy, *Les Chroniques et annales de France dès l'origine des François & leurs venues ès Gaules,* 1600.
> Cormerius, T. *Rerum gestarum Henrici II Regis Galliae libri quinque,* 1584.
> Corrozet, G. *Les Antiquitez, croniques et singularitez de Paris, Ville capitale du Royaume de France . . . ,* 1586 (with a "liure second" . . . "recueillies par Jean Rabel, Parisien," 1588). See also Corrozet's edition of 1550.
> Paradin, Guillaume. *Histoire de nostre temps . . . ,* 1555.
> Pasquier, Estienne. *Recherches de la France,* in Amsterdam edition of the *Oeuvres,* 1723, 1, col. 701.

Saulx, G. de, Seigneur de Tavannes. *Mémoires,* n.p, n.d.

Sleidanus, Ioannes, *De Statu Religionis et reipublicae, Carolo Quinto, Caesare, commentariorum,* pars altera, Strassburg, 1555, fol. 567.

Vieilleville, F. de. *Mémoires* in *Collection complète des Mémoires relatifs à l'histoire de France,* ed. M. Petitot, 26, 302–10.

VIII Modern studies of the Entry

Bryant, Lawrence M. *The French Royal Entry Ceremonial: politics, art and society in Renaissance Paris.* Ph.D. dissertation, University of Iowa, 1978.

Champion, Pierre. *Paganisme et Réforme,* in his series *Paris au temps de la Renaissance,* 1936, especially Chapter X.

Chartrou, J. *Les Entrées solennelles et triomphales à la Renaissance,* 1928.

Gébelin, F. "Un manifeste de l'école néo-classique en 1549: L'Entrée de Henri II à Paris," *Bulletin de la Société de l'Histoire de Paris,* 51(1924): 35–45.

Huon, Antoinette, "Le Thème du Prince dans les entrées parisiennes," *Les Fêtes de la Renaissance,* ed. J. Jacquot, 1956, 21–30.

Saulnier, V.-L. "L'Entrée de Henri II à Paris et la révolution poétique de 1550, ibid., 31–59.

IX The artists involved

a. Contemporary works:

Relevant translations by Jean Martin:

Horapollo, *De la signification des notes hieroglyphiques des Aegyptiens,* J. Kerver, 1543. BL, BN

(I have also used the 1553 edition, likewise published by Kerver, under the title *Les Sculptures ou graueures sacrées.)* BL, OB

Il primo libro . . . Le premier livre d'Architecture de Sebastien Serlio . . . 1545 OB

(This edition includes Martin's translation of Books II and V as well as the Italian text of Books III and IV.)

Hypnerotomachie ou Discours du Songe de Poliphile, J. Kerver, 1546. BL, BN, OB

Architecture ou Art de bien bastir de Marc Vitruve Pollion Autheur Romain antique, J. Gazeau, 1547. OB

L'Architecture de bien bastir du Seigneur Leon Baptiste Albert, J. Kerver, 1553 BL, OB

Cousin, Jehan. *Livre de Perspectiue,* Iehan le Royer, 1560.
                                                        BL, BN, OB
De l'Orme, Philibert. *Le premier tome de l'architecture,* F. Morel, 1568.
                                                        BL, OB

b. General:

Béguin, Sylvie. *L'Ecole de Fontainebleau. Le maniérisme à la cour de France,* 1960.

Blunt, A. *Art and Architecture in France 1500–1700,* 1953, second ed. 1957.

————· *Philibert de l'Orme,* 1958.

Dimier, L. *Le Primatice, peintre, sculpteur et architecte des rois de France,* 1900.

Du Colombier, P. *Jean Goujon,* 1949.

Dupuy, P. "Jean Goujon et son rôle comme architecte sous Henri II," *Bulletin de la Société nationale des Antiquaires de France,* 1912, 209–15.

Guiffrey, J. *Les Artistes parisiens des XVIe et XVIIe siècles,* 1915.

Laborde, L. de. *Les Comptes des bâtiments du roi (1528–1571),* 2 vols. 1877–80.

————· *La Renaissance des Arts à la cour de France,* 1886.

Mantz, Paul. "Recherches sur l'histoire de l'orfévrerie française," *Gazette des Beaux-Arts,* Series 1, 9 (1861) 15–41.

Marcel, Pierre. *Jean Martin,* 1927.

Roy, Maurice. *Artistes et monuments de la Renaissance en France,* 2 vols in one (continuous pagination), 1929–34. This work includes the reprint of the article "Collaboration de Philibert de l'Orme aux préparatifs de l'entrée de Henri II à Paris," *Revue du seizième Siècle,* 5 (1917–18): 209–33; information on Jehan Cousin, and *passim* on various craftsmen employed for the Entry (Laurent Constant, Guillaume de Saint-Jorre, Luc Penni, etc.).

Strong, Roy. *Splendour at Court: Renaissance Spectacle and Illusion,* 1973.

Thieme, U., Becker, F. and collaborators. *Allgemeines Lexikon der bildenden Künstler,* 1 (1907)–36 (1947), Leipzig.

X Contemporary works relevant to certain aspects of the Entry

Alciat, A. *Emblematum libri duo,* Lyon, J. de Tournes & G. Gazeau, 1547.   OB

Cartari, V. *Les images des dieux des anciens* . . . , trans. Antoine du Verdier, 1606 (first Italian edition, 1556).　　　　BL, BN, OB

Choul, Guillaume du. *Discours de la Religion des anciens Romains,* Lyon, G. Rouille, 1556.　　　　BL, BN, OB

Comes, Natalis (Conti). *Mythologie ou explication des fables* . . . , trans. J. Baudoin, 1612 (first Italian edition, c. 1551).　　　　BN, OB

Fulvio, Andrea. *Opera* . . . *della antichità della Città di Roma,* Venice, 1543.　　　　OB

Giovio, P. & Symeoni, G. *Dialogo dell'Imprese militari et amorosi,* Lyon, G. Rouille, 1574.　　　　OB

Giraldi, L.G. *De Deis Gentium varia & multiplex Historia,* Basel, Oporinus, 1548.　　　　OB

Paradin, Claude. *Les Devises heroiques,* Lyon, J.de Tournes & G. Gazeau, 1571.　　　　OB

Valeriano, G. P. *Les Hieroglyphes* . . . , Lyon, P. Frellon, 1615 (first Italian edition, 1556).　　　　OB

XI MODERN WORKS RELEVANT TO CERTAIN ASPECTS OF THE ENTRY OR TO OTHER FRENCH ROYAL ENTRIES

Allen, D. C. *Mysteriously meant,* Baltimore & London, Johns Hopkins, 1970.

Asher, R. E. "Myth, legend and history in Renaissance France," *Studi Francesi* 39 (1969): 409-19.

Bardon, Françoise. *Diane de Poitiers et le mythe de Diane,* 1963.

Blunt, Anthony. *Artistic Theory in Italy, 1450-1600,* 1968.

Chamard, Henri. *Histoire de la Pléiade,* 4 vols., 1939-40.

Courbon, F. *Histoire illustrée de la gravure en France,* vol. 1, 1923.

Demerson, Guy. *La Mythologie classique dans l'oeuvre lyrique de la Pléiade,* Geneva, 1972.

Dubois, Cl.-G. *Celtes et Gaulois* . . . *avec l'édition d'un traité de Guillaume Postel, De ce qui est premier pour réformer le monde,* 1972.

Gelli, J. *Divise, Motte e Imprese di famiglie & personnaggi italiani,* Milan, 1928.

Giesey, Ralph E. *The Royal Funereal Ceremony in Renaissance France,* Geneva, 1960.

Gluck, Denise. "Les Entrées provinciales de Henri II," *L'Information d'histoire de l'art* 10 (1965): 215-18.

Graham, V. & McAllister Johnson, W. *The Parisian Entries of Charles IX and Elizabeth of Austria, 1571,* Toronto and Buffalo, 1974.

Guenée, Bernard & Lehoux, Françoise. *Les Entrées royales*

françaises de 1328 à 1515, 1968.

Henkel, A., & Schöne, A. *Emblematik. Handbuch zur Sinnbildkunst des XVI. und XVII. Jahrhunderts,* Stuttgart, 1967.

Joukovsky, Françoise. *La Gloire dans la poésie française et néo-latine du XVIe siècle,* Geneva, 1969.

Jung, M.-R. *Hercule dans la littérature française du XVIe siècle,* Geneva, 1966.

Kernodle, George R. *From Art to Theatre: Form and Convention in the Renaissance,* Chicago, 1944.

Lalanne, L. *The Book of Fortune.* Two hundred unpublished Drawings by Jean Cousin, trans. H. M. Dunstan, 1883.

McCrary, Ronald G. *Native Tradition and Classical Revival in French Renaissance Triumphal Entries,* Ph.D. dissertation, University of Missouri, 1974.

Panofsky, Dora and Erwin. *Pandora's Box: the changing Aspects of a mythological Symbol,* New York, second ed. 1965.

Seznec, Jean. *The Survival of the Pagan Gods,* London & New York, 1953.

Simone, Franco. "Une entreprise oubliée des humanistes français: de la prise de conscience historique du renouveau culturel à la renaissance de la première histoire littéraire," in *Humanism in France,* ed. A. H. T. Levi, Manchester & New York, 1970, pp. 106–31.

Tervarent, G. de. *Attributs et symboles dans l'art profane 1450–1600. Dictionnaire d'un langage perdu,* Geneva, 1958 (*Supplément et Index,* Geneva, 1964).

Tourneur, V. "Les origines de l'Ordre de la Toison d'or et la symbolique des insignes de celui-ci," *Bulletin de la Classe des Lettres et des Sciences morales et politiques,* Académie Royale de Belgique, 5th series, 42 (1956), 300–23.

Wind, Edgar. *Pagan Mysteries in the Renaissance,* 1967.

Livret

of the

King's Entry

C'eſt l'ordre qui a eſte te-

NV A LA NOVVELLE ET IOYEVSE

entrée, que treshault, treſexcellent, & treſpuiſſant
Prince, le Roy treſchreſtien Henry deuzieme
de ce nom, à faiɕte en ſa bonne ville & cité de Paris, capitale de ſon Royaume,
le ſezieme iour de Iuin
M.D.XLIX.

On les vend à Paris par Iehan Dallier ſus le pont ſainɕt
Michel à l'enſeigne de la Roſe blanche.

PAR PRIVILEGE DV ROY.

HENRY *par la grace de* Dieu Roy de France, *aux* Preuoſt de Paris, ſe-
nechal de Lion, *&* à tous noz autres iuſticiers *&* officiers *qu'il appartiĕ-
dra, ou à leurs lieutenants* ſalut *&* dilectiō. ſcauoir uous faiſons que nous
inclinãt liberalemĕt à la ſupplication *&* requeſte, qui faicte nous a eſté de
la part de noſtre biĕ aimé* Iaques Roffet, *dit le* Faulcheur, *imprimeur iuré de
noſtre bōne uille *&* cité de* Paris, à iceluy pour ces cauſes auons permis *&*
octroyé, permettons *&* octroyōs de grace ſpeciale, plaine puiſſance *&* au-
ctorité Royale par ces preſentes, qu'il ſeul puiſſe *&* luy loiſe imprimer *&*
expoſer en uĕte le traicté qui ſera faict *&* cōpuſé de la ioyeuſe *&* nouuelle
entrée de nous, *&* de noſtre treſchere et treſaimée compagne la* Royne, *en
noſtre* dicte uille *&* cité de* Paris. Et ce durant le temps *&* terme d'un an
durant, commenceant au iour *&* dacte de la premiere impreſſion qui ſera
faicte dudict traicté, ſans ce que pendant ledict temps d'un an autres imprimeurs que luy les puiſſe imprimer ne faire imprimer, uendre ne expoſer
en uente, en quelque maniere que ce ſoit. Si uoulons *&* uous mandons, *&*
à chacun de uous, ſi comme à luy appartiendra, que de noz preſens per-
miſſion *&* octroy, *&* de tout le cōtenu cy deſſus, uous faictes, ſouffrez *&*
laiſſez ledict* Roffet *ioyr *&* uſer plainement *&* paiſiblement. En faiſant
faire expreſſes inhibitiōs *&* deffences de par nous, ſur certaines *&* grãdz
peines à nous à appliquer, A tous libraires, imprimeurs, *&* autres qu'ils
n'ayent à imprimer, ne faire imprimer ledict traicté, ne iceluy expoſer *&*
faire expoſer en uente, comme deſſus eſt dict. En procedant par uous cōtre
ceulx qui ſeront trouuez faiſans le contraire, cōme contre infracteurs de
noz ordonnances *&* deffences,* Car tel eſt noſtre plaiſir. *Donné à* Chantilly *le dernier iour de* Mars, L'an de grace Mil cinq cens quarante huict, *&*
de noſtre regne le deuxieme.*

Par le Roy.

Duthier

C'eſt l'ordre qui a eſte te-

NV A L'A NOVVELLE ET IOYEV-
ſe entrée, que treshault, treſexcellent, & treſpuiſſant
Prince le Roy Treſchreſtien Henry deuxieme de ce
nom à faiđe en ſa bonne ville & cité de Paris, capitale de ſon Royaume, Le ſezieme iour de Iuin M.
D. XLIX.

ET PREMIEREMENT,

ES Preuoſt des marchás & Eſcheuins
de ladiđe ville, ayans eſté aduertiz par
Móſeigneur de la Rochepot, Cheualier
de l'ordre, & gouuerneur de l'iſle de
Fráce, que lediđ Seigneur Roy treſchreſtien auoit deliberé faire ſon entrée en
ſadiđe ville de Paris, & celle de treshaulte & treſilluſtre Dame Madame Catherine de Medicis ſon eſpou-
ſe, enuiron lediđ mois de Iuin. Pour la ſumptuoſité &
magnificence de ladiđe entrée, & afin de faire clere &
ouuerte demonſtration de la ioye & lieſſe incroyable
qu'ils receuoyent, de la nouuelle venue en ladiđe ville
de leur ſouuerain & naturel Seigneur, firent eriger &
dreſſer aucuns arcs de triumphe, & autres manufađu-
res, d'excellent artifice, ſubtile & louable inuention,
tant à la porte de ladiđe ville nommée la porte Sainđ
Denis, que au dedans dicelle ville, ainſi qu'il eſt cy apres
eſcrit.

A ladiđe porte ſainđ Denis, par laquelle lediđ Sei-

a ii

gneur entra fut fait vn auāt portail d'ouurage Tuſcā &
Dorique, dedié à la Force, pour faire entendre que dedans Paris conſiſte la principale force du Royaume. Et
pour venir à la deſcription de ceſt auāt portail, ſon diametre par terre eſtoit de douze piez en largeur, l'ouuer
ture de dixneuf de hault, ſur huit de large, & de trois
toiſes deſpoiſſeur. Aux deux coſtez des piles eſtoyent
deux ſtilobates ou piedeſtalz de proportion diagonée,
enrichiz de conuenables moulures, ſurquoy eſtoyēt po
ſez deux grās Colloſſes d'hommes, veſtuz à la ruſtique,
portans treze piez en haulteur, mis en lieu de colonnes
Perſanes ou Cariatides. Leurs baſes Doriques entie-
rement couuertes d'or,cōme auſſi eſtoyent leurs chapiteaux. Iceulx Coloſſes tenoyēt entre leurs mains chacū
vn grand croiſſant d'argent, pour le moins de cinq piez
en diametre, dedans leſquels eſtoit eſcrit en lettre Ro-
maine noire,D O N E C T O T V M I M P L E A T
O R B E M,qui eſt la deuiſe du Roy.

Par deſſoubs les panneaux de ioinᴁ de la Ruſtique,
terminans la circunferéce de l'arc,paſſoyent l'architraue,la frize,& la cornice,dōt les extremitez ſe pouuoyēt
veoir deſſus les chapiteaux. Dedás le plat fons du frontiſpice eſtoit vn grād eſcu aux armes de la ville, enrichy
de deux branches de Palme, pour emplir le vuyde du
tympan:& ſur ce frontiſpice eſtoit leué vn ſode,ou bien
face quarrée painᴁe de pierre de mixture,dedás laquelle y auoit vn Cartoche à lantique, ſouſtenu par deux
mannequins aſſis, & appuyans leurs gauches ſur le gla-
cis de la couronne d'iceluy frontiſpice. Et ſur le champ
de ce Cartoche couché de noir, eſtoit eſcrit en lettre
d'or, T R A H I M V R, S E Q V I M V'R-
Q V E V O L E N T E S. Hemiſtiche,certes,cō-
uenant

uenant merueilleufemét bien à quatre perfonnages, en
profil, plus grans que le naturel, efleuez fur ce fode, veftuz feló leur qualité, affauoir vn en la maniere que l'on
voit ordinairemét noz Euefques & Prelats, aufsi reprefentoit il l'Eglife: vn autre armé à l'antique, portant cy-
meterre au cofté, fignifiant Nobleffe: le tiers veftu de
robbe longue, denotãt confeil: & le quart habillé en vi-
gneron tenant vne houe en fa main, qui demõftroit labeur. Ces quatre faifoyent contenãce de marcher fran-
chement, & à grans pas, les mains tédues deuers vn Her
cules de Gaule eftant de front au milieu deux, dont le
vifage fe rapportoit fingulierement bien à celuy du feu
Roy Francois, Prince clemét en iuftice, reftaurateur des
bons arts & fciences, mefmes plus eloquent que autre
qui ait regné en Fráce deuát luy. C'eft Hercules eftoit
veftu de la peau d'un Lyõ, les pattes nouées fur l'extre-
mité du bufte pour cacher la partie que cõmãde nature,
& tout le refte du corps nu. En fa main dextre il tenoit
en lieu de maffue vne lance entortillée d'un ferpét, re-
couuert d'un rameau de Laurier, fignifiãt que prudence en guerre eft occafion de victoire. En la gauche tenoit fon arc, & portoit en efcharpe vne groffe trouffe
pleine de fleches. de fa bouche partoyent quatre chaif-
nettes, deux d'or, & deux d'argét, qui s'alloyét attacher
aux oreilles des perfonnages deffus nommez: mais elles
eftoyent fi treflaches, que chacun les pouuoit iuger ne
feruir de contrainéte: ains qu'ils eftoyent voluntairemét
tirez par l'eloquence du nouuel Hercules, lequel a faiét
fleurir en ce Royaume les lãgues Hebraique, Grecque,
Latine, & autres, beaucoup plus qu'elles n'ont iamais
faiét par le paffé. A la clef de c'eft arc pédoit vn tableau
à fons noir enrichy de ce quatrin efcrit en lettres d'or.

Pour ma doulce eloquence & royale bonté,
Chacun prenoit plaiſir à m'honorer & ſuyure:
Chacun voyant auſsi mon ſucceſſeur m'enſuyure,
L'honore & ſuit, contrainct de franche volunté.

Le berceau de c'eſt auant portail eſtoit par tout enrichi de groſſes poinctes de diamant fainctes, qu'il faiſoit
merueilleuſemét bon veoir, & ſes flács reparez deſcuſ-
ſons aux armes du Roy & de la Royne, enuironnez de
chapeauz de triumphe, qui auoyent bien fort bonne
grace.
　　Au fons de ce berceau & droictement ſur l'entrée de
la ville, y auoit vn autre tableau de meſme façon & lettre que la precedente, ou ſes mots eſtoyent eſcrits,
Ingredere, & magnos, aderit iam tempus, honores
Aggredere.
　　Mais pour ne plus tenir les lecteurs en ſuſpens, & leur
faire congnoiſtre toutes ces particularitez par teſmoi-
gnage oculaire il leur eſt preſenté cy endroit la figure
de c'eſt auant portail.

Au dedans de ladicte ville à la Fontaine du Ponceau, qui est en la rue Sainct Denis, y auoit vn autre spectacle veritablemét singulier: c'estoyent trois Fortunes de relief beaucoup plus grandes que le naturel. La premiere d'or, la secóde d'argent, & la tierce de plób, asises soubs vn Iupiter de dix piez en haulteur, planté sur vn globe celeste, tenant son bras droit cótremont, & maniát son fouldre sur la paulme de sa main, en cótenance gracieuse, & toutesfois redoutable, tenát en sa gauche son sceptre, pour demonstrer sa puissance au ciel, en la mer, en la terre, & aux abysmes.

Ceste premiere Fortune representoit celle du Roy, et du Royaume, à raison dequoy luy fut baillé tout expres vn gouuernail en dextre, pour donner à entendre que tout demeure soubs son gouuernemét. De só bras gauche elle embrassoit vne corne d'abondance, la gueulle tournée cótre bas, d'ou sortoit pluye d'or, signifiát que toutes manieres de richesses sont en la maiesté Royale.

La seconde estoit celle des nobles, armée en Amazone, tenant vne targue en sa senestre, & de sa droicte faisant monstre de tirer son espée hors du fourreau, pour donner à cógnoistre qu'elle est tousiours appareillée à offendre ou deffendre, ainsi que le bon plaisir du Roy gouuerné par raison, est de le commander.

La tierce denotoit celle du peuple, & tenoit sa main droitte dessus son estomach, en signe de fidelité et d'innocence : en la gauhe portoit vn coultre de charue, & des aisles au doz, pour manifester à chacun sa diligence tousiours laborieuse. Vray est que les deux precedentes n'en auoyent point, pour donner à congnoistre leur

immobilité,

immobilité, & par efpecial de celle du Royaume, qui portoit en fon mot en lettre d'or fur fons d'azur, appliqué en la frize du mafsif de la fontaine, REGNO-RVM SORS DIVA COMES.

Celuy de la feconde en mefme forme & reng eftoit, SORS FIDA POTENTVM.

Et l'autre de la tierce continuant en pareille ligne & femblables caracteres, IMPIGRA IVSTA-QVE SORS PLEBIS. Apres le Iupiter difoit, TIBI SCEPTRA IOVEMQVE CONCILIANT.

Et au pilaftre Ionique canellé regnant deffus le refte des deux principales faces de l'hexagone, côftituant l'edifice de la Fontaine, y pendoit vn autre tableau enrichy de ce quatrin.

Le grand Romain fa louange autorife,
Du fort fatal de fa profperité:
Mais plus d'honneur a le Roy merité,
A qui fort triple & vn Dieu fauorife.

Quant aux autres ornemens de platte painɛture, accommodez aux faces de la maffonnerie, & au d'oremét des moulures qui fe monftroyent de bonne grace, n'en fera cy faiɛte mention, remettant aux leɛteurs d'en faire iugement par la figure cy prefente.

b

Paſſant oultre ladicte fontaine du Ponceau, & venāt deuant ſainct Iacques de l'hoſpital, ſe trouuoit vn grād arc triumphal à deux faces, d'ordre Corinthien, conduict auecques toutes les proporcions & beaultez artificieles qui appartiennent à tel ouurage. L'ouuerture auoit quatorze piez ſur vingtſix de hault, & les piles de deux coſtez en eſpoiſſeur ou profondeur comprenoyent trois toiſes de meſure: les piez d'eſtalts eſtoyent iuſtement d'un quarré parfect auec deux tiers, ſur chacun deſquels ſe releuoyent deux colónes de Corinthe, canelées & rudentées, qui portoyent vintgquatre piez en longueur, depuis l'empietement iuſques au diametre d'enhault. Leur renflement pris ſur la tierce partie & demie de toute la tige meſurée en ſept diuiſions egales. Les baſes faignoyent le marbre blanc, come en ſemblable faiſoyent leurs chapiteaux tant bien taillez & reueſtuz de leurs fueilles d'acanthe ou branque vrſine, qu'ils ſembloyét à la veue esblouyſſante par trop les cō templer, qu'elles vndoyaſſent au vent. La rudenture de ces colonnes eſtoit expreſſement bronzée par ſi excellent artifice, que ceſtoit choſe fort exquiſe. Deſſus les chapiteaux regnoyent l'architraue, la frize, & la cornice, ou n'y auoit vn ſeul point à redire: meſmes ceſt ar chitraue eſtoit perlé & billetté par ſi bonne induſtrie ſuyuāt la vraye antiquité, qu'aucun ouurier ou autre bō eſprit entendant l'architecture, n'en euſt ſceu reporter que grand contentement. Quant a la frize ſon fons du coſté de la porte ſainct Denys, premierement ſubiect à la veue du Roy, eſtoit d'or: & les maſques releuez auec les fleurons de deſſus, auſſi blācs que marbre poly, au moyen dequoy ils tenoyent en admiracion les yeulx de tous les regardans.

b ii

Deſſus la clef de l'arc poſoit vne Gaule couronnée de
de trois tours, pour repreſenter ſesparties, à ſcauoir l'A-
quitanique, la Belgique, & la Celtique, portant ſes cheueulx eſpars ſur les eſpaules & monſtrant vn regard
tant venerable entremeſlé de doulceur gracieuſe, que
tout le monde en eſtoit reſiouy.

Elle tenoit en ſes mains des fruicts & fleurs de main-
te ſorte de ſa production, pour demonſtrer l'heureuſe
fertilité qui luy eſt ottroyée par le createur, telle & ſi
grande que toutes les nations prochaines & loingtai-
nes le peuuent aſſez teſmoingner.

Son accouſtrement eſtoit d'un drap d'or azuré, tant
bien ſeant à ſa facture que rien mieulx, & ſoubs ſes piez
repoſans deſſus vne groſſe poincte de dyamant, eſtoit
eſcrit en lettre noire ſur le blanc,

GALLIA FERTILIS

Deſſus le retour des cornices y auoit deux petiz enfans nuz, repreſentans le marbre, couchez & acoudez
de bonne grace ſur deux cornes d'abondance, pareillement remplies de tous fruictaiges, voulans denoter que
la Gaule eſt mere commune à tous peuples. Entre ces
deux figures ſe releuoit vng ſode en lieu de frontiſpice,
dedãslequel eſtoit eſcript en lettres d'or ſur fons d'azur

Terra antiqua, potens armis, atque ubere glebæ,
Terna tibi populos Gallia mater alo.

Sur ce ſode eſtoyét formez deux Anges pour le moins
de dix piez de hault: & toutesfois pour la haulteur du
lieu ou ils eſtoyent aſsis, reuenoyent quaſi en proportió
naturelle. Ils tenoyent de leurs mains droictes vn eſcu
de France

de France,au fons d'azur,à trois fleurs de lis d'or,taillez
de relief.Cest escu estoit enuironné & enrichy d'un collier de l'ordre sainct Michel à double rég de coquilles,
qui luy donnoyent vn singulierement beau lustre.

Les gauches de ces Anges esleuées portoyét vne cou
róne Imperiale pour vray timbre de cest escu,en signi-
fiance que le Roy des Francois ne recongnoist aucun su
perieur en terre, ains est monarque en son pays , qu'il
ne tient sinon de Dieu & de l'espée.

Telle estoit la premiere face de cest arc, dont l'entredeux des colonnes estoit garny des armoiries du Roy
& de la Royne, mises en chapeaux de triomphe.Et sur
les timpans entre la circonference du berceau & le plat
fons de l'architraue, volletoyent par semblant deux
Victoires d'or, tenans en leurs mains droictes chacune
sa couronne de Laurier,& aux gaulches vn rameau de
Palme. Puis dedans les piedestals y auoit deux tableaux à l'antique,pour la dedicasse de l'arc, adressans à la
Gaule fertile, en l'un desquels estoit escrit en lettres
d'or sur vn fons noir,

MATRI PIAE,& en l'autre POPVLORVM
OMNIVM ALVMNAE S. D.

Le reste des piles estoit diapré de pierre de mixture,
tant bien faincte du naturel,que l'œuure s'en monstroit
admirable.

Voila en somme quele estoit la premiere face
de cest Arc, duquel le fons du berceau fut paré d'un
compartiment de moresque à grosses rosaces d'or,

auec les deuifes & chiffres du Roy,les parquets reparez
de feftons de Lyerre qui donnoyent vn grand efgaye-
ment à toute la befongne.

Dedans les flancs y auoit deux quarrez de platte
painéture,veritablement faiéte de main de maiftre : en
l'un dequels fe uoyoit la reprefentation du fleuue Seine portant couróne de laurier . Il eftoit demy couché,
demy leué fur deux rofeaulx aquatiques , & tenoit
en l'une de-fes mains vn auiron, pour monftrer qu'il
eft nauigable , & de l'autre s'accoudoit fur vne hydrie
dont fortoit de l'eaue en abondance tele qu'il s'en faifoit vne groffe riuiere : fur les borts & terrouers de laquelle fe voyent plufieurs nymphes fes filles,qui refpan
doyent leurs vafes en fon canal,à fin de la plus augmé-
ter.Le paifage fe monftroit doulx & entremeflé: & les
traiéts menez par induftrieufe perfpeétiue, abufoyent
tellement la veue,qu'elle eftimoit veoir bien loing en
pais.Ce neantmoins la fuperficie en eftoit toute vnie.

Le goulet de l'vrne de ce fleuue s'enuironnoit d'une
pancarpe ou fefton de tous fruiéts,par efpecial de blez
& de raifins, pour monftrer la fertilité prouenante de
fon cours.

En la platte bande ou ceinéture regnant au niueau
des moulures du pié d'eftal,tout autour du maffif, y a-
uoit vn efcriteau de lettres d'or, à fons d'azur contenant ces mots,

FOELIX SEQVANAE VBERTAS.
A l'autre

A l'autre flanc ou cofté fe monftroit vn pareil fleuue repréfentát la riuiere de Marne, dont ie laiffe la defcription:nonobftant que la figure ne cedaft à la premiere, pour auoir efté faicte toute d'une mefme main : mais pour euiter prolixité, ce fleuue portoit pour fa deuife,

GRATA MATRONAE AMOENITAS.

En l'autre face de l'arc eftant de femblable manufacture que la premiere, excepté que le fons de la frize eftoit couché de blanc,& les mafques auec les fleurons tresbié eftoffez d'or pour diuerfifier la mode,fur la clef à l'oppofite de la Gaule,feoit vn bon Euenement veftu d'un habit fimple, tenãt en fa main droicte vne couppe d'or, & en l'autre vne poignée d'efpiz de blé fuyuant la defcription des antiques. Deffoubs fes piez eftoit efcrit en lettre noire fur le blanc,ne plus ne moins que foubs la Gaule.

BONVS EVENTVS.

A fes deux coftez fur les retours des cornices gifoyét aufsi au côtredos des deux enfans,Flora& Pomona bié belles , acouldées Flora fur vn caniftre plain de fleurs tenant en main vn vray lis naturel, & Pomona deffus vne vrne propre à enrofer iardins, maniant de bonne grace vne ferpette commode à effarter les arbres.

En droicte ligne du grant efcu de France,tenu par les deux Anges,comme deffus eft dit,pofoit fur le fode vn Zephyrus regardant deuers l'Eglife du fepulchre,& foufflant par deux trompes antiques contre Flora & Pomona,pour donner à entendre que la trefdoulce alaine de ce vent leur eft fingulierement proffitable.De-

dans ledict ſode y auoit deux vers latins auſsi en lettre
d'or, ſur fons d'azur, de la teneur ſuyuante.

Quum tibi tot faueant fœcundæ numina terræ,
Adſum ego, & euentis cuncta ſecundo meis.

Et pource que en vn ſeul quatrin n'euſt ſceu eſtre có-
priſe la ſignification de ces deux faces, fut conſtruit &
mis ſoubs les piez de la Gaule un double tableau, dedás
lequel furent eſcrits en lettres d'or ſur vn fons noir
ces vers qui enſuyuent,

L'antique Cybele gloire produict aux Dieux,
Et preſte abondamment ſubſtance à la nature:
Moy Gaule, ie produy honneur & nouriture
Au Roy, à ſes ſubiects, & hommes de tous lieux.
　　　Puis en l'autre y auoit,
Flore promet par ſon mari Zephyre
De fruicts & fleurs heureux euenement.
Le Roy promet par ſon aduenement
Le vray bon heur ou toute France aſpire.

De la premiere face de ceſt Arc ſe peult veoir cy la figure, qui ſuffit aſſez pour la ſeconde, à raiſon que l'ouurage eſt tout de meſme, mais non l'inuention des perſonnages faincts, qui ſemblent aſſez exprimez pour
gens de bon entendement.

Deuát l'Eglife du Sepulchre qui eft aufsi en ladicte rue
fainct Denys,y auoit vne merueilleufe aiguille trigona
le,portant foixante dix piez en haulteur depuis fon rez
de chaufeé,non cóprins en ce l'empiétement qui eftoit
dedans terre plus de fept piez en profond,la ftructure
& compofition de laquelle merite bié d'eftre aucune-
ment celebrée. A cefte caufe ie dy que fur fondict rez
de chaufée elle eftoit circuye d'un ftilobate ou piede-
ftal de neuf piez & demy de hault, portant vingt en lógueur,fur toife & demie de large, painct en tous fes qua
tre coftez de pierres fainctes de porphyre,iafpe, ferpen-
tine,& autres,que l'antiquité a grandement recommá-
dées,& que nous tenons encores au iourd'huy en grád
pris,à raifon de leur naïue beauté , laquelle toutesfois
n'empefchoit que ces faces ou coftez ne feuffent enrichiz des armes du Roy & de la Royne, enuironnez de
chapeaux de triumphe,enfemble de Croiffans,doubles
H H,& autres chiffres de fa maiefté, qui diaproyent les
brodures tout à l'entour, & augmentoyent grandemét
la bonne grace de la befongne.

Deffus le plan de ce perron pofoit la figure d'un animal d'Ethiopie nommé Rhinoceros,en couleur defcor
ce de buys,armé d'efcailles naturelles , ennemy mortel
de l'elephant,& qui de faict le tue en fingulier combat,
nonobftant qu'il ne foit pas du tout fi hault,mais bien
egal en fa longueur.Chofe que fon ouurier ayant con-
fidereé,luy dóna dixhuit piez deftendue,foubs vnze de
montée. Et au milieu du dos luy appliqua vne baftine
bien affermie de deux fangles,furquoy ceft animal fembloit porter ce qui furmontoit de l'aiguille , laquelle e-
ftoit en toutes ces trois faces enrichie de compartimés

dorez fur le fons de porphyre. Et en la principale y a-
uoit vn grand quarré côtenant les veuz des Parifiés en
hieroglyphes,que ie reciteray apres auoir prealablemét
dit que tout au fefte de cefte aiguille,fur vn globe doré,fut plantée vne Fráce de dix piez en haulteur, armée
à l'antique, reueftue d'une togue Imperiale azurée &
femée de fleurs de lis,faifant contenáce de remettre fon
efpée au fourreau,comme victorieufe de plufieurs ani-
maulx cruelz & fauuages,qui gifoyent detrenchez &
morts deffoubs le ventre de ce Rhinoceron . A la veri-
té on y pouoit veoir des lyons, des ours, des fangliers,
des loups, des regnars & autres telles beftes rauiffan-
tes fouldroyées du triple fouldre partant du globe feruant de marchepié à cefte feconde Bellona, pour figni
fier aufsi confirmation de veuz , & lequel eftendoit fes
flammes tout au long des faces du trigone facré. Chofe
qu'il faifoit merueilleufement bon veoir:& encores qui
eft plus à confiderer,cefte France auoit pour fon mot,
Q V O S E G O,Puis pour la côfecration de l'aiguille
en vn quarré eftoit efcrit de lettre d'or fur fons d'azur,

HENRICO II. REGI P. F. A. P. P.

ADVENTVS NOVI ERGO,
CIVES LVTETIANI VOVERVNT.
D. D. Q.
ANNO M. D. XXXXVIIII.

Au bas de l'aiguille pres le doz du Rhinoceró, eftoit
efcrit en Grec, ΑΛΕΞΙΚΑΚΟΣ ,qui vault autát à dire
comme en domtant les monftres,ou mauuais.

Mais pour n'oublier les hieroglyphes , Premierement il y auoit vn lyon & vn chien de front, repofans
chacun vn pié fur vne couronne de France Imperiale,
eftant au milieu d'eulx vn liure antique fermé à gros
fermoirs, dedans le liure vne efpée nue trauerfante de
bout en bout:vn ferpent tortillé en forme de couleu-
ure,vn croiffant large,duquel les cornes repofoyent fur
deux termes:vn globe fur marche d'un pié tiré du natu
rel,vne poupe de nauire & vn trident, vn oeil ouuert,
vnes fafces confulaires , vn rond ou cercle , vn pauois,
vne ancre de lóg,deux mains croifées fur des rameaux
d'oliuier:vne corne d'abondance, deffus laquelle tom-
boit pluye d'or,vn cerf,vn d'aulphin, vne couronne de
l'aurier,vne lampe antique allumée,vn mors de cheual,
& puis le timon d'un nauire , qui fignifioyét en s'adref
fant au Roy,Force & vigilance puiffent garder voftre
Royaume:Par confeil,bonne expedition, & prudence
foyent voz limites eftenduz , fi qu'à vous foit foubmife
toute la ronde machine de la terre,& que dominez à la
mer, ayant toufiours Dieu pour vengeur & deffenfeur
contre voz ennemys:par ferme paix & concorde,en af
fluence de tous biens longuement & fainement trium
phateur,viuez,regiffez & gouuernez.
   En la premiere face du ftilobate y auoit vn tableau
placque, dedans lequel eftoit efcrit en lettre d'or , fur
vn fons noir,ce quatrin difant en la perfonne de Fráce,
   Longuement a vefcu,& viura la memoire
   D'Hercules,qui tant a de monftres furmontez:
   Les peuples fiers & forts par moy France domtez
   Furent,font & feront ma perdurable gloire.
Telle eftoit la dedication de ce trigone facré à la maiefté Royale. Mais à fin que la figure fupplie à ce qui
pourroit auoir efté omis,elle eft icy reprefentée.

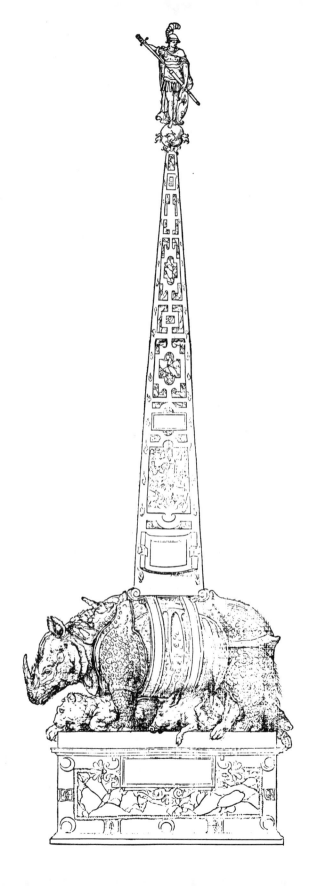

Plus oultre fur main droicte fe trouuoit la fontaine
fainct Innocent de nouueau rebaftie d'un ouuraige fin
gulier, enrichy de figures de Nymphes, fleuues & fon-
taines à demy taille, enfemble de feuillaiges fi artificiel-
lement vndoyans & refenduz, qu'il n'eft pofsible de l'ex
primer en petit de parolles, parquoy en eft laiffé le iugement àceulx qui de prefent la peuuent veoir, & s'enten
dét en tels ouurages. Ladicte fótaine eftoit embellie dedás euure de diuerfes damoifelles & bourgeoifes, auec
plufieurs gentils hommes & citoyés de la ville, tant bié
en ordre que ceftoit toute beauté .

Peu de chemin apres fe reprefentoit deuát le Chafte-
let, en la place nómé l'Apport de Paris , vn autre fpecta
cle de platte painðture, qui n'eft pas à laiffer en arriere.

C'eftoit vn portique à la mode Ionique, proprement
dipterique, c'eft à dire garny d'ailes, ou double reng de
colonnes, tant en fa principale rencótre qu'en fon fons,
dont l'eftendue eftoit de fix toifes & demye en largeur,
foubs cinq autres & demye de hault : lefdictes colónes
glacées de toutes les pierres de meflange que la nature
peult produire: & pour telle diuerfité l'euure en eftoit
infiniemét plus beau. Leurs bafes & chapiteaux repre-
fentoyent le bronze felon la maniere de plufieurs antiques . Chofe qui leur donnoit vn trefgrant ornement.
Par deffus regnoyent l'architraue, la frize, & la cornice
de proportion bien obferuée.

Deffus le plá de ce portique y auoit vne Lutece appel
léepar fó inuétaire la nouuelle Pádora, veftue en Nym
phe, les cheueux efpars fur fes efpaulles, & au demeurát
treffez

treſſez à l'entour de ſa teſte, d'une merueilleuſement
bonne grace : elle eſtoit agenouillée ſur vn genoil côme pour faire honneur au Roy à ſa reception, & faiſant
contenance d'ouurir de l'une de ſes mains vn vaſe antique ſeulement remply de tous les heureux preſens des
puiſſances celeſtes, non des infortunez, mis iadis en celuy de la facture de Vulcan, & tenant lautre main leuée
en l'air, comme pour rendre la maieſté Royale atentiue
à ſon dire, qui eſtoit vn quatrin eſcrit en lettre d'or ſur
vn fons noir contenant ces parolles :

Iadis chacun des Dieux feit vn double preſent
A la fille Vulcan qui s'en nomma Pandore.
Mais, Sire, chacun d'eulx de tous biens me decore :
Et puis qu'a uous ie ſuis, tout eſt voſtre à preſent.

Ce tableau eſtoit affiché contre deux colonnes po-
ſantes ſur le plan d'un eſcallier, par ou l'on euſt penſé
monter audit portique, tant il eſtoit bien ordonné, & les
traicts naiuement menez par induſtrie : meſmes le iour
& l'ombre en furent ſi bien touchez à limitation du naturel, qu'il n'eſt pas poſsible de mieulx. Et quât à la maſ
ſonnerie releuée ſur ledict plan, il n'y auoit coing de ba
ſe, n'y de chapiteau qui ne ſe rapportaſt au vray poinct
du milieu, au moyen dequoy ſe réfondroyent & releuoyent les membres par ſi grande apparence, que meſmes pluſieurs ouuriers expers euſſent iugé qu'il y auoit
grande ſeparation entre la figure & le baſtiment, en la
frize duquel eſtoit eſcrit en lettre d'or ſur fons d'azur,

SOSPES TE SOSPITE VIVAM.

Et en vn tableau fainct de relief au deſſus de la teſte
de ceſte Pandora, y auoit auſsi eſcrit en lettre d'or,

LVTETIA NOVA PANDORA.

Aux colonnes de ce portique, pendoyent de beaux
feſtons de verdure, ou eſtoyent attachées les armes du
Roy, & de la Royne, enuironnées de chapeaux de triumphe, dont la diſpoſitió du fueillage emulateur de la
nature, donnoit vn ſouuerain plaiſir à tous. Et encores
pour mieulx perſuader que tout l'ouurage eſtoit maſſif,
celuy qui en feit l'ordonnáce, dreſſa au deſſus de la cornice vne gallerie hypæthrique, ou à deſcouuert, perſée
à iour, laquelle mettoit beaucoup de gens en doubte, à
raiſon qu'ils pouuoyent veoir l'air commun par à trauers. Choſe qui grandement aidoit à l'artifice, dont le
deſſeing eſtoit ſemblable à ceſte monſtre.

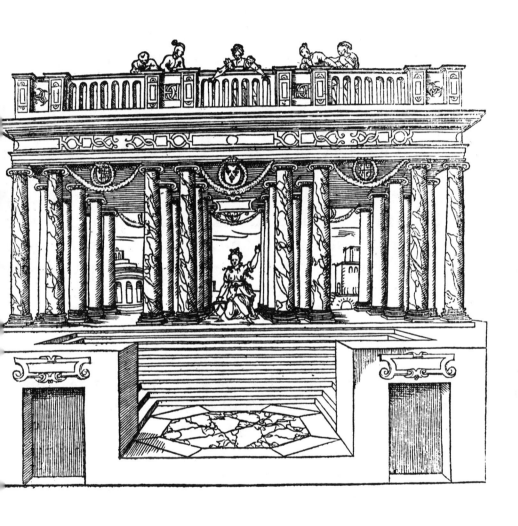

Au bout du Pont noſtre Dame eſtoit vn arc triũph-
phal de l'ordre compoſé,contenant quatre toiſés de lar
ge , en ce compris les piles , dont l'ouuerture du milieu
auoit vnze piez de diametre,ſoubs vingtdeux de hault,
& vne bonne toiſe deſpoiſſeur. Le berceau en fut enrichy d'un compartimét d'argét embouty ſur fons noir,
qui ſont les couleurs Royales , leſquelles luy donnerét
grand luſtre.

Deſſus la circunference du demy rond, regnoit vn
architraue auec ſa frize , aorné de groz bouillons de
fleurs,& ſa cornice de moulures conuenables à ſa mode, ſur le plan de laquelle eſtoit dreſſé vng plinthe bas,
reſpódant à plomb du nu de l'arc, ou ſe pouuoit veoir
debout vn Typhis de dix piez en ſtature,dont la figure
approchoit bien fort de celle du Roy triumphateur,&
tout le reſidu bien formé , ayant pour couurir la partie ſecrette vn flocart de lierre ceinct au deſſus de ſes
hanches.

En ſes deux mains il tenoit vn grand maſt de nauire,
garny de hune & d'un grand voile de taffetas rayé d'ar
gét. A ſa dextre y auoit vn Caſtor argenté,& à ſa ſene-
ſtre vn Pollux tout noir, plus grans que le naturel, &
toutesfois ſemblans petiz au pres de la grande corpu-
lence de leur pilotte. Le Caſtor tenoit en l'une de ſes
mains vne grande eſtoile noire , & le Pollux vne d'argent,pour deſigner l'immortalité ou renouuellement
de vie:& aux deux autres tenoyent chaſcun ſon ancre,
ſignifians aſſeurance en nauigation.

Dedans quatre niches faicts expres,a ſcauoir deux de
chacun

chacun cofté contre la principale face de ceft arc, &
encauez iufques à la feptieme partie de fon maſſif, y a-
uoit quatre des plus fameux Argonautes veftuz à l'antique, & garniz de leurs auirons, chacun faifant contenance diuerfe, dont les noms eftoyens Telamon & Peleus, auec Hercules & Hylas.

Puis en l'autre face y en auoit vn pareil nombre de
platte painéture, tant bien defignez & mis en couleur,
qu'ils ne cedoyent à ceulx de relief, ceftoyent Thefeus
& Pyritous auec Zetus & Calaïs. Tous lefquels pour
eftre de nation gregoife, difoyent à leur Typhis apres
Homere,

ΗΜΕΙΣ ΕΜΜΕΜΑΩΤΕΣ ΑΜΈΥΟΜΕΟΑ.

Qui fignifie, Nous defireux & prompts te voulons fuy-
ure enfemble. Ce mot eftoit en la circóference de l'arc,
en caraéteres conuenables à la langue.

Contre les flancz, tant d'un cofté que d'autre, y auoit
deux tableaux, en l'un defquels eftát à la main droéte,
on pouoit veoir Phryxus confacrant au dieu Mars la
toifon d'or de fon mouton, fur quoy il auoit trauerfẽ
le Bofphore de Thrace, ou fa feur Hellé fe noya, laif-
fant fon nom à cefte mer, qui deflors iufques à prefent
en a efté diéte Hellefponte: Sur ce Phryxus eftoit fon
nom efcrit en lettre d'or, & foubs fes piez,

QVOD MARTI PHRYXVS SACRAVERAT.

En l'autre y auoit vn Iafon rauiffant ladiéte peau d'or
& emmenant Medée. Au bas duquel eftoit aufsi efcrit

pour refpondre au premier, A B S T V L I T A R T E
A E S O N I D E S. Puis en s'adreſſant au Roy, T V
M A R T E F E R E S. Et dedans le plinthe ſoubs les
piez du Typhis ſe pouoit lire en lettre d'or, ſur fons d'a-
zur ce ver de Virgile diſant,

Alter erit iam Typhis, & altera quæ uehat Argo
-Delectos heroas.

Pareillement au milieu de ceſt arc y pendoit vn cartoche garny de ce quatrin,

Par lantique Typhis Argo fut gouuernée,
Pour aller conquerir d'or la riche toiſon:
Et par vous Roy prudent à ſemblable raiſon,
Sera noſtre grand nef heureuſement menée.

Cela eſtoit dict au Roy, pour autant qu'il eſt gouuerneur de la nef de Paris, nõ inferieure à l'anciéne Argo.
Quant aux autres particularitez de ceſte architecture,
la figure cy apres miſe y ſatisfera.

Ce pont noſtre Dame a enuiró ſoixante quinze toiſes de long , & en chacun de ſes coſtez ſont ſituées tré-
te quatre maiſons toutes marquées de lettres d'or, ſur
fons rouge, par nombre entreſuyuant depuis la premie
re iuſques à la derniere : ſur les diuiſions deſquelles au
ſecond eſtage y auoit des Sereines de boſſe plus grandes que le naturel, belles par excellence, qui haulſoyent
leurs bras contremont, & en chacune main tenoyent
un feſton de lierre montant par deſſus le tiers eſtage,
dont ſe faiſoit vn cópartimét ſingulier, lequel couuroit
le pont tant de long que de large, & en eſtoyent les en-
trelaz enrichiz des deuiſes du Roy, ſcauoir eſt de dou-
bles H H d'or , ſur fons d'azur , de Croiſſans d'argent,
ſur fons noir, de fouldres , & arcs à corde rompue,
couchez ſur vn plat fons, dont les extremitez faictes en
demy rond, eſtoyent garnies de teſtes de Meduſe, criá-
tes par ſemblát à bouche ouuerte, & treſſées en lieu de
cheueulx de petiz ſerpenteaux, couchez de verd de terre, tortillez en facon de neu ſur le ſommet de chacune
des teſtes, ainſi qu'a ſuffiſance lexprime la figure.

A l'autre bout dudict pont se trouuoit vn second
arc estát de semblable ordre & artifice que le premier,
mais different de figures & inuention. A la face du dedás euure qui se presentoit en veue la premiere, y auoit
contre les piles quatre niches fainéts de platte paincture, dedans chacun desquels estoit planté de bóne grac
vn demydieu, ou demydeesse, des plus renómez de l'antiquité, singulieremét en l'exercice d'archerie. Ceulx l
estoyent Calisto & Archas, auec Croton & Pandarus
tant bien exprimez au naturel, que l'on ne se pouoit a
souuir de les regarder: leurs noms estoyent escrits des
soubs leurs piez, & en la face principale, que les pas
sans auec sa maiesté n'eussent sceu veoir sans tourne
les visaiges en arriere. Se trouuoyent ordonnez dans l
massif quatre autres niches rempliz de pareil nombr
de figures de relief, chacune representant son dieu, de
my dieu, ou deesse, dont les noms furent, Genius Prin
cipis, beau & ieune, comme de dixhuit ans, mais fort a
prochant l'effigie du Roy : Iris messagere de Iuno, &
les deux Cupidons, l'un grand sans bádeau & sans ai
les ainsi que Platon le descrit, & l'autre petit, aueugle
en la forme que les painctres ordinairement le nou
presentent, lesquels tenoyent aussi chacun son arc a
poing comme prests à le báder, & en tirer pour le ser
uice du Roy triumphateur : acte que faisoyent pareill
mét vn Phœbus & vne Phœbé, l'un d'or & l'autre d'a
gent de dix piez en haulteur, plantez dessus le plinthe
posé sur la cornice, ne plus ne moins que le Typhis, &
ses collateraux dessus l'arc precedent, appuyans chacu
l'une de ses mains sur vn globe terrestre estant au mi
lieu d'eux, & disans à la maiesté Royale le distique e
scrit en lettre d'or, à fons d'azur, en la maistresse fac
de c

de ce plinthe.

Vnde orimur terris, terris ubi condimur iifdem,

Hic regni duplex terminus efto tui.

A l'entour de la circuferéce du berceau y auoit pour tous ces archiers, efcrit en lettre noire fur fons blác, AR TI PRAETENDIMVS ARCVM. Mefmes dás le cartoche pendát à plób de fon centre, pour denoter l'intention de l'inuenteur y auoit ce quatrin efcrit:

Sire, croyez puis que de fi bon cueur

Pour voftre nom perpetuer fe bande

De demy dieux & dieux cefte grand bande,

Que des vainqueurs vous ferez le vainqueur.

Dedás les flács du fufdiét arc y auoit des tableaux, en l'un defquels fe pouoit veoir vne Aurora de vifage ver meil, couronnée de rofes, veftue en Nymphe, afsife fur des nues obfcures que les rayós du foleil Oriét faifoyét peu à peu difparoir parmy la fpatiofité de l'air. Elle e-toit du bras gauche accoudée fur vne tefte de beuf fei-che, pour denoter le retour au labeur: & tenoit en fa maí droitte vne lampe allumée, fignifiát la lumiere du iour approchante de noftre hemifphere. Deffus fa tefte eftoit fon nom efcrit en lettre d'or, & foubs fes piez,

A ME PRINCIPIVM.

A l'autre flác eftoit vn Hefperus, pareillemét afsis fur des tourbillós de nuages engrofsifïás par les vapeurs ter reftres, luy portát la face endormie tournée côtrebas, la perruque noire & pédáte, mefmes tenát fes bras croifez fur fon giró, cóme ne demádát que le repos. Só accou-tremét eftoit aufsi rougeaftre, couuert d'ú máteau noir femé d'eftoilles peu apparoiffantes, excepté vne qui ré-doit grád clarté. Il auoit femblablemét fon nom deffus fa tefte, & foubs fes piez ce mot, MIHI DESINET.

c

Chofes qui auoyent efté faictes expres, à fin de ne laiffer mufer le peuple en vain, deuãt ny apres l'entrée dudict Seigneur Roy.   Voyla en fomme quel fut l'artifice, inuention & intelligence des deffufdicts ouurages,
refte à venir au faict & ordre de ladicte entrée.

LE SEZIEME iour dudict mois de Iuin , le Roy
arriua enuirõ les huit heures du matin, au Prieuré
fainct Ladre lez Paris , ou luy auoit efté dreffé vn
efchauffault tenãt au logis du Prieur dudict fainct Ladre, pour y ouir & receuoir les harengues & faluta-
tions qui luy feroyent faictes de la part de ceulx de ladicte ville , & pour garder que en cela ny euft preffe ne
cõfufion, & que ceulx qui feroyét montez fur ledict efchauffault pour leffect que deffus, ne nuififfent aux autres qui les fuiuroyét, l'on y feit deux efcaliers , l'un qui
feruit à mõter, & l'autre à defcédre. & fut ledict efchauf
fault couuert de riche tapifferie, & au milieu d'iceluy té
tendu vn dez foubs lequel fe pofa la chaize dudict Seigneur, couuert d'un riche tapiz de veloux pers, femé de
fleurs de lisde fil d'or traict, pour y feoir ledict Seigneur.

Vne bõne heure & demye ou enuirõ apres fõ arriuée
audict lieu, cõmécerét à marcher au deuãt de fa maiefté
les quatre ordres médiánes, & fuyuant eulx les Eglifes.

Apres fuyuit l'Vniuerfité de Paris, au mefme habit &
ordre qu'elle a toufiours fait de bonne & anciéne cou
ftume es autres entrées des Roys.

Ceulx la paffez vint le corps de la ville en l'ordre &
equipage cy declaré, à fcauoir de deux à trois mil hommes de

mes de pié,choifiz & efleuz des dixfept meftiers de ladi
&te ville,côdui&s par leurs capitaines & lieutenás,leurs
enfeignes au milieu,tous brauemét accouftrez des couleurs du Roy & de la Royne,les aucuns armez de cor-
celets & morrions la plufpart dorez & grauez ,portás
vne partie hacquebuttes , & les autres piques & hallebardes , acompagnez de phiffres & tabourins en bon
nombre,felon qu'il eft de couftume entre gés de guerre
tels qu'ils fe monftroyent.

Suyuans ceulx la,marcherent les Imprimeurs tous habillez de noir ayans plumes blâches,& equippez en gés
de guerre , lefquels eftoyent en nombre de trois cens
cinquâte ou enuiron:la plufpart portans animes,corfe-
etz , morrions dorez & enrichiz , & les autres maillez,
eftans côdui&z de leurs capitaine,lieutenât,& cap d'ef-
quadre dudi&t eftat,richement armez . Marchans trois
trois,leur enfeigne de blâc,noir,& incarnat au milieu,
efquelz faifoit bon veoir.

Apres fuyuoyent les menuz officiers de ville à pié,iuf-
ques au nôbre de cent cinquâte,reueftuz de robbes my-
arties de drap rouge & bleu, les chauffes de mefme,
portás chacun vn bafton blâc au poing,& eftoyét con-
ui&s par deux fergés de ladi&te ville à cheual,habillez
ôme eulx,finon que pour la difference ils auoyent d'a-
âtage fur les mâches gauches de leurs robbes,chacun
n nauire d'argent, qui font les armoiries de la ville.

A leur doz marcherent à cheual les cent archers de
di&e ville, habillez de leurs hocquetons d'orfeurerie
ux armes d'icelle ville,ayans la plufpart les manches &

bas de leurs fayes de veloux couuerts & enrichiz d
broderie & boutons d'or, marchás deux à deux,& de
uant eux trois trompettes , leurs capitaine, guidon &
enseigne, & auoyent chacun la pertuisane en la main.

Les six vingts haquebutiers vindrét apres en mesm
ordonnance & parure, garniz chacun de sa haquebu
à larson de sa selle & du feu en la main.

A leur queue les soixante arbalestiers en semblab
ordonnance & habits , portans aussi comme les a
chiers vne pertuisane au poing.

Ces trois compagnies passées, se móstrerét six ving
ieunes hommes, enfans des principaux marchans
bourgeois de ladicte ville códuicts par leurs capitain
lieutenant, enseigne,& guidon, habillez de sayes à d
my manches de veloux noir,recouuert de broderie
fueillages & deuises de fil d'or & d'argent , le vuide
leurs accoustremés remply de pierreries, perles, fers
boutons d'or . Ceulx de leur troupe estoyent parez
mesme , & oultre la braueté de leurs accoustreme
dont la valleur en estoit bien fort grande,ilz estoye
couuerts de chemises de maille auec morrions en tel
la pluspart d'argent, & les autres richemét dorez & l
bourez , tous garniz de grans pennaches des couleu
du Roy & de la Royne,& qui n'est à omettre, n'y auc
vn seul d'eulx qui ne fust monté sur vn cheual d'Esp
gne ou autre braue cheual de seruice,capperassonné
semblable parure que son saye, le cháfrain fourny de
naches de pareille couleur que celuy de son morrion
comme on peult veoir en la figure qui s'ensuyt.

Ceſte cõpagnie fut ſuyuie par les maiſtres des euu res
de charpéterie & maſſõnerie, auec le capitaine de l'artil
lerie de Paris, & vne troupe de ſergés fort bié habillez.

Apres eulx marcha maiſtre Claude Guiot, conſeil-
ler, notaire, ſecretaire du Roy, & côtrerolleu r de l'au-
diéce de la Chãcellerie de France, lors Preuoſt des mar
chans de la ville, habillé de robbe mypartie de veloux
cramoyſi brun, & veloux tanné, & de ſaye de ſatin cramoyſi, monté ſur vne mulle enharnachée d'un harnois
de veloux noir frãgé d'or, la houſſe bãdée à grãdes bã-
des trainãtes en terre, ayant à coſté de luy le plus ancien
Eſcheuin de ladiๆe ville, & à ſa ſuitte les autres Eſcheuins & le greffier, habillez de pareilles robbes. Le procureur de leur congregatiõ eſtoit apres, paré d'une rob
be toute de veloux cramoyſi rouge, & ſuyuant luy les
ſeize conſeilliers dicelle ville, habillez de robbes longues de ſatin noir, doublées de veloux noir, marchans
tous deux à deux.

Les deſſuſdiๆs auoyét à leur queue ſeize Quartiniers
de ladiๆeville portás robbes de ſatin tãné, & à leur doz
les maiſtres iurez des meſtiers, à ſcauoir quatre gardes
de la draperie, veſtuz de robbes de veloux noir: quatre
eſpiciers, de veloux tanné : quatre merciers, de ueloux
violet: quatre pelletiers, de robbes de veloux pers fourrez de loups ceruiers: quatre bõnetiers, de veloux tãné,
& quatre orfeures, de veloux cramoyſi. & eſtoyent leſ-
diๆs iurez à l'aller ſuyuiz d'un grand nombre des prin
cipaux deſdiๆs meſtiers habillez diuerſement, mais au
retour ils porterent le poiſle & ciel de parement ſur la
Maieſté du Roy, chacun à ſon tour, ainſi qu'il ſera decla
ré cy apres.

Ceulx la paſſez,vint le Cheualier du guet auec ſon gui
don,ſes lieutenát & ſergés du guet tous à cheual, habil
lez de leurs hocquetons d'orfeurerie à leurs deuiſes ac-
couſtumées,qui eſt vne eſtoille ſur le deuant & derriere
de leurſdiᵭs hocquetós,portans chacun vne pertuiſane
en la main.

Suyuant eulx les vnze vingts ſergens à pié,en bonne
ordonnance,diuerſement & richement accouſtrez.

Apres eulx les quatre ſergens fiefez, à cheual.

A leur queue les notaires,habillez de robbes lógues
noires,& de ſayes de veloux ou ſatin,& ſuyuát eulx les
commiſſaires du Chaſtellet en meſme parure.

Apres les ſergens de la douzaine,à cheual habillez de
hocquetons d'orfeurerie à la deuiſe du Roy, qui eſt vn
croiſſant couronné.
Tous les deſſuſdiᵭs paſſez,vint le Preuoſt dudiᵭ Paris brauement armé,& habillé de ſaye de drap d'or,enri
chy de canetilles & cordós d'or, les bardes de ſon cheual de meſme,& auoit deuant luy ſes deux pages habillez de ſayes de veloux tanné, faiᵭs à broderie,ſon eſcuyer au milieu, tous montez ſur cheuaux d'Eſpagne.

Lediᵭ Preuoſt eſtoit ſuyui des trois lieutenás,ciuil,
criminel,& particulier, & des aduocats & procureurs
du Roy audiᵭ Chaſtelet,portans robbes deſcarlatte,&
deſſus chapperons de drap noir à longue cornette , &
ſuyuant eulx des Conſeillers,& apres leſdiᵭs Conſeillers, les plus notables Aduocats & procureurs audiᵭ
Cbaſtelet.

Apres eulx se trouuerent les sergés à cheual, leur enseigne & guidó deuát eulx, habillez de cazaquins de ve
loux, ayás l'une des máches aux couleurs, deuises, & chif
fres du Roy, tenans chacun la pertuisane en main.

Le corps de la ville passé en la sorte & ordonnance
que dessus, quelque peu de temps entredeux les gens de
Iustice commencerent à marcher.

ET premierement les Generaux des mónoyes, leurs
quatre huissiers allans deuát, & apres lesdicts huissiers
leur greffier. Le President desdicts generaux estoit ha
billé de robbe de satin noir, & lesdicts Generaulx de
robbes de damas, & a leur queue auoyent les officiers
de la monnoye & les changeurs.

Suyuant eulx furent les Generaulx de la Iustice des
aides, precedez par leurs huissiers, & leur greffier habillé de robbe d'escarlatte, auec son chapperó de drap
noir à lógue cornette. Les deux Presidens estoyét parez
de robbes longues de veloux noir, & les Generaulx &
Conseillers desdicts aides, de robbes descarlatte, portás
ausi dessus leurs chapperós de drap noir à lógue cornette, & auoyét à leur queue les Esleuz des aides & tail-
les en l'election de ladicte ville, reuestuz de robbes de
damas.
Messieurs de la chambre des comptes vindrét conse
cutiuement, ayans leurs huissiers deuant eulx: & suyuát
lesdicts huissiers leurs deux greffiers habillez de robbes
de damas. Les presidens de ladicte chambre estoyét reuestuz de robbes de veloux noir. Et les Maistres & au
diteurs des comptes, de robbes de satin & damas.

Messeigneurs

Meſſeigneurs de la court de Parlement ſouueraine de ce Royaume,marcherét apresen leur ordre accouſtu mé,leurs huiſſiers deuát eulx.Et ſuyuát leſdicts huiſſiers les quatre notaires & greffier criminel & des preſenta- tions de ladicte court, veſtuz de robbes deſcarlatte. Le greffier ciuil apres eulx ſeul portant ſa chappe fourrée de menu ver. Apres luy & deuant les Preſidens de ladicte court, le premier huiſsier auſsi ſeul habillé deſ- carlatte,ſon mortier de drap d'or en la teſte, fourré de menu ver eſpuré.

Les quatre Preſidens eſtoyent reueſtuz de leurs chap pes deſcarlatte,leurs mortiers en la teſte en la maniere accouſtumée: Ayant Monſieur le premier Preſident ſur leſpaule gauche de ſa chappe, trois petites bandes de toille d'or pour la difference des autres preſidens.

A leur queue eſtoyent les Cóſeillers tant laiz que ec- cleſiaſtiques,auec les deux Aduocats,& au milieu d'eulx le Procureur general, tous portans robbes deſcarlatte, leurs chaperons de meſme fourrez de menu ver.

A meſure que tous les deſſuſdicts paruindrét au lieu de ſainct Ladre, ils trouuerent le Roy ſur l'eſchauffault qui auoit eſté dreſſe, accompagné des Princes, Cheua- liers de ſon ordre,& autres grans ſeigneurs qui ſeront cy apres nommez, & meſmement à ſes deux coſtez Meſſeigneurs les Conneſtable & Chácelier de France. Et apres luy auoir faict la reuerence,& ainſi qu'il eſt de couſtume,faict propoſer par les principaux d'entre eulx leurs harengues , & meſmes le Preuoſt des marchans preſenté audict Seigneur les clefz de ladicte ville,ils s'en retournerent au meſme ordre quils en eſtoyent partiz,

f

referué Monſeigneur le Preuoſt de Paris qui demeura
auec le Roy, & marcha en la troupe des gentils hommes de la chábre,enſemble auſsi quelques vns de Meſ-
ſieurs des aides,des comptes,& de la court de Parlemét,
leſquels cheminás par la rue ſainɛt Denys ,ſe retirerent
es maiſons de leurs parés & amys,pour veoir auec plus
de commodité ladiɛte entrée.

Les deſſuſdiɛts retournez cóme deſſus eſt recité,le Roy
fut ſalué par ladiɛte ville, de trois cens cinquante piè-
ces d'artillerie, & peu de temps apres commencerent à
marcher ceulx qui eſtoyent de ſa ſuyte & compagnie.

Premierement Meſſeigneurs les Maiſtres des Reque
ſtes,habillez de robbes de veloux noir,ayans deuát eulx
les deux maiſtres d'hoſtel de Móſeigneur le Chácelier,
reueſtuz de robbes de damas,bádées à grádes bádes de
veloux faiɛtes à broderie.Suyuant leſdiɛts Maiſtres des
Requeſtes,eſtoyét les deux huyſsiers de la Chancelerie,
portás robbes de veloux cramoyſi violet,& leurs maſſes
au poing. A leur doz les Audiencier de Fráce & cómis
du Contrerolleur de l'audience,à raiſon que pour lors
lediɛt Cótrerolleur eſtoit Preuoſt des marchans, parez
de robbes de veloux noir, & puis eſtoit le Seel du Roy
en ſon coffret, couuert d'un grand creſpe, poſé ſur vn
coiſſin de veloux pers , ſemé de fleurs de lis d'or,por-
té par vne hacquenée bláche couuerte d'une houſſe de
veloux pers,auſsi ſemée de fleurs de lis d'or trainát iuſques en terre. Ladiɛte hacquenée eſtoit menéé par deux
laquetz de Móſeigneur le Chácellier,habillez de pourpoints & chauſſes de veloux cramoyſi,& coſtoyée par
les quatre Chauffecires , reueſtuz de robbes de veloux
cramoyſi,

cramoyſi, qui portoyent les courroyes dudiât ſeau, ayãs eulx & leſdiâs laquaiz les teſtes nues.

Suyuât iceluy Seel marchoit Módiâ Seigneur le Chã cellier, veſtu de robbe de drap dor frizé ſur champ cra-moyſi, monté ſur ſa mulle, enharnachée d'un harnois de veloux cramoyſi brun, frágé d'or, & couuert de bou cles d'or, la houſſe de meſme parure, ayant à ſes deux coſtez quatre laquaiz habillez comme les deux prece-dens. Apres luy eſtoit l'vn de ſes Eſcuyers, auec l'un de ſes Secretaires, portans robbes de damas.

Mondiâ Seigneur le Châcellier paſſé en l'ordre que deſſus, ſuyuit Berthelot l'un des Preuoſts des mareſ-chaux de France, au gouuernemeñt de Champagne & Brie, auec ſes lieutenans, greffiers & archiers.

Apres vindrent les pages des Gentils hommes ſer-uans du Roy, & à leur queue ceulx des Gentils hom-mes de la chambre, Capitaines, Contes, & autres grans Seigneurs, & penſionnaires meſlez enſemble: & puis des Cheualiers de l'ordre, & ſuyuant eulx, des Mareſ-chaulx & Conneſtable de France, enſemble des Prin-ces eſtans auec le Roy, montez ſur courſiers, rouſsins, cheuaux Turcs, & d'Eſpaigne, portans en leurs teſtes les vns les armets, & aux mains les lances de leurs mai-ſtres, garnyes au bout de banderolles aux couleurs du Roy, & les armets de grans & riches pennaches. Les autres portoyét morriós fourniz de meſme, auec leurs ródelles & corſeſques. Leſdiâs cheuaux eſtoyent bra-uement & richement enharnachez, vne partie bardez,

f ii

& l'autre caparaſſonnez , mais tous de diuerſes ſortes,
ſe rapportans toutesfois la pluſpart aux habillemés des
pages qui les cheuaulchoyent , qui eſtoyent aux vns de
drap d'or,aux autres de drap d'argent,& veloux de diuerſes couleurs, brochez d'or, ou faicts à broderie, aux
couleurs & deuiſes de leurſdicts maiſtres,& tous ſi pro
prement & de ſi bonne grace,qu'ils ne donnerét moins
d'admiration que de plaiſir & contentement aux yeulx
de tous ceulx qui les veirent.

A leur queue marcherent les deux Preuoſtz de l'hoſtel,auec leurs lieutenans & procureurs du Roy,leurs
greffiers, & tous leurs archers, veſtuz de leurs hocquetons d'orfeurerie à la deuiſe du Roy , qui eſt vn croiſſant couronné,ayant vne eſpée au milieu, pour la difference des autres archers de la garde dudict Seigneur,&
auoyét leſdicts archers chacun la pertuiſanne au poing.

Ceulx la paſſez vindrént pluſieurs ieunes gentils hómes & ſeigneurs , habillez de draps d'or & d'argent,
chacun à ſa deuiſe: & à leur queue les gentils hommes
ſeruans,armez de riches harnois d'hommes d'armes,
veſtuz par deſſus de ſayes de veloux noir , couuerts de
broderie à fueillages de toille d'argent , & leurs cheuaux bardez de meſmes.

Apres eulx les Gentils hommes de la chambre, auſsi
armez & parez de ſayes de toille d'argent , enrichiz de
broderie à fueillages de veloux noir, & parmy eulx plu
ſieurs Contes,Capitaines,& autres grans ſeigneurs &
perſonnages , auſsi armez & richement habillez . Et
fait icy à noter que le Sieur de Chemault Preuoſt de l'or
dre &

dre & maiſtre des ceremonies, ayant à l'entrée de la ville diſpoſé chacun ſelon ſon ordre, eſtant ſuyui de dix
archers de la garde alloit ca & la, pour faire entretenir
& garder ledict ordre.

Suyuant les deſſuſdicts Seigneurs, Capitaines, & Gentils hommes, vindrent les Cheualiers de l'ordre, portans leurs grans ordres au col, auſsi armez & diuerſement acouſtrez:mais tous les deſſuſdicts Gentils hommes, Côtes, Capitaines, & Cheualiers, auec telle braueté & richeſſe tant en harnois, accouſtremens, que chapeaux, la plus part couuerts de pierreries, que pource
que la choſe ſeroit par trop longue & difficile à repreſenter cy par le menu, ie me contenteray de dire qu'il
euſt eſté bien malaiſé d'y pouoir rien adiouſter, ſoit de
valeur ou d'inuention, & auſsi peu aux harnois & pennaches de leurs cheuaux, meſmes aux bardes qui toutes ſe rapportoyent aux habillemés des ſeigneurs eſtans
deſſus.

Les deuant nommez furent ſuyuiz des cent Suyſſes
de la garde, veſtuz de pourpoints & chauſſes eſcartel-
lées, moitié de toile d'argent, & moitié de veloux noir,
leurs bonnets couuerts de grans pennaches à leur mode, aux couleurs du Roy, & furent conduicts par Móſeigneur de la Marche filz aiſné de Móſeigneur le Mareſchal de la Marche capitaine deſdicts cent Suyſſes, lequel tenoit le lieu de ſondict pere, & eſtoit habillé à la
façon deſdicts Suyſſes, de pourpoint & chauſſes de toile d'argent. Apres luy eſtoit le Lieutenát d'iceulx Suyſſes, reueſtu de meſme parure, le page dudict Seigneur
de la Marche portant ſemblable accouſtrement que

f iii

lefdicts Suyffes , menoit deuant luy fon petit cheual io-
liement enharnaché , & tenoit en fa main les efperons
de fon maiftre.

Cefte bende paffee en fort bon ordre,ainfi qu'il leur
eft de couftume,vindrét à cheual les Phiffres & Trompettes du Roy, fonnans de leurs inftrumens , habillez
de fayes de veloux noir , bandez à grandes bandes lar-
ges de toile d'argent.

Suyuant eulx les Heraux & leurs pourfuyuans, veftuz de leurs cottes d'armes.

Apres treze pages d'honneur, montez fur treze cheuaux du Roy,diuerfement & trefrichement enharnachez. Lefdicts pages habillez de pourpoints,& haults
de chauffes de fatin blác decouppé, & de fayes à demies
máches, de veloux blanc,couuerts de broderies de cordons d'argent, les bonnets de veloux blanc, garniz de
plumes blanches.lefdicts pages eftoyent fans efperons,
& auoyét les pallefreniers & marefchaux de l'efcuyrie à
cofté d'eulx, veftuz de chamarres de damas blanc, &
haults bonnetz de mefmes. & fault noter que les deux
derniers pages eftoyent montez fur deux Turcs blancs,
caperaffonnez de mefme l'habillemét du Roy,l'un portát fon morrion, de pareille facó que fon harnois,auec
vne rondelle delicatement labourée & grauée d'or bra-
zé deffus,fa corfefque en la main,& l'autre l'armet aufi
de mefme facon,l'un & l'autre garniz de grans pennaches enrichiz d'or.

A leur queue eftoit le Sieur de Carnaualet, l'un des
Efcuyers

Efcuyers d'Efcuyrie, môté fur l'ū des cheuaux du Roy, portant deuant luy le manteau Royal.

Apres luy le Seigneur de Sipierre, qui portoit le cha- peau Royal.

Le Seigneur de Genli le troifieme auec les gātelets.

Et le Seigneur de Caluoifin premier Efcuyer, le der- nier, portant l'armet Royal, couuert du mantelet Roy- al de veloux pers, femé de fleurs de lis d'or traiȼt, four- ré d'hermines mouchetées, & couronné d'une couró- ne clofe.

Et n'eft à omettre que tous les deffufdiȼts Efcuyers, e- ftoyét habillez, & leurs cheuaux bardez de toile d'argét noire, enrichie de broderies d'argét aux deuifes du Roy.

Les Seigneurs de Sedan & de fainȼt André Maref- chaux de France, eftoyent apres richement armez & parez de fayes de drap d'or frizé, bordez d'un large bord de fatin cramoyfi, couuert de groffes canetilles d'or, leurs cheuaux portans bardes pareilles.

A leur queue venoyent à pié les fommeliers d'armes dudiȼt Seigneur, veftuz de fayes de veloux noir.

Suyuant eulx le cheual de parade du Roy, entiere- ment couuert d'un grand caperaffon de veloux pers, fe- mé de fleurs de lis d'or traiȼt, trainant en terre. Il por- toit au cofté droit de l'arfon de fa felle, la maffe dudiȼt Seigneur Roy, & de l'autre part fon eftoc, & eftoit lediȼt

cheual mené par deux Efcuyers d'efcuyrie , allans à pié
ainfi qu'il eft de couftume.

Monfeigneur de Boyfi grand Efcuyer de France mar
choit apres, armé & môté fur vn autre cheual du Roy,
couuert de mefme capperaffon que ledict cheual de pa
rade:il portoit en efcharpe l'efpée de parade du Roy,&
auoit les caualcadours à pié, aupres de luy.

Le Sire de Montmorancy premier Baron & Conneftable de France, venoit confecutiuement, tenant l'efpée
de Conneftable nue en la main, armé d'un harnois fort
richement doré & labouré , habillé par deffus d'un
faye de drap d'or frizé, enrichy d'une bande large faicte
à gros fueillages enleuez de toile d'argent, frizée, femée
d'efpées nues, & de fourreaux & ceinctures de veloux
pers , enrichies de fleurs lis d'or, qui font les deuifes de
Conneftable, le refte de l'abillement de groz fueillages
enleuez de toile d'argent frizée, & eftoit monté fur vn
braue courfier portant bardes pareilles à fon faye.

L A maiefté du Roy precedée par tous les deffufdicts,
eftoit foubs vn ciel de veloux pers, femé de fleurs de lis
d'or traict, à franges de mefmes, couuert de fes armes,
chiffres & deuifes, qui fut porté premierement par quatre Efcheuins de la ville , depuis la porte dudict fainct
Denys, iufques deuant l'Eglife de la Trinité:& dela iufques deuant l'Eglife de fainct Leu fainct Gilles , par les
quatre gardes de la draperie de ladicte ville, feconds en
ordre, qui le mirent es mains des quatre maiftres Efpi-
cies, lefquels le porterent depuis icelle Eglife de fainct
Leu fainct Gilles, iufques à fainct Innocent:ou les Merciers

ciers le receurent,& depuis le deliurerét aux Pelletiers,
qui s'en acquiterent iufques deuant le Chaftellet: & la
les Bonnetiers le vindrent prendre pour en faire leur
deuoir iufques à fainɗ Denys de la chartre,ou ils le deliurerét aux Orfeures,qui le porterent iufques à noftre
Dame,& encores depuis iufques au Palais.

Lediɗ Seigneur eftoit armé d'un harnois blanc,poly
fubtilement, & delicatement graué, furgetté d'or dans
la graueure,qui luy donnoit diuers luftres, & paré par
deffus d'un faye de drap d'argent frizé,excellent & fort
riche,garny d'un bord large de frizós faiɗs de canetille
d'argét, à fes chiffres & deuifes, le demourant du fayê
decouppé & r'ataché de boutons & guippures d'argent, d'eftrange & nouuelle facon, doublé d'une toile
d'argent qui auec fa beauté rendoit vn grand efclat, fa
ceinɗure eftoit d'argent ferrée d'or, & la garniture de
fon efpée tout de mefme,enrichie de plufieurs rubiz &
diamans,fon chapeau de fatin blanc,couuert de caneti-
le d'argét,auec vn pénache blanc,femé de grand nóbre
de perles,& pour enfeigne vn grand diamát, auec trois
perles pendátes, dót oultre l'excelléce & perfeɗion de
beaulté, la valeur s'en difoit ineftimable. Il eftoit monté fur vn beau & braue courfier blanc,bardé de mefme
parure que fon faye, & autant bien voltant & bondif-
fant qu'autre que l'on ait iamais veu.

Lediɗ Seigneur auoit deuant luy fes laquaiz,habillez
de pourpoints & chauffes de toile d'argét,& apres eulx
feze Efcuyers d'Efcuyrie,fans les deux qui menoyent
fon cheual de parade, reueftuz de fayes de toile d'argét
bádez de bádes d'argét veloutées deverd.ils marchoyét

g

à pié, & portoyent tous botines blanches, & efperons dorez au pié, les haults de chauffes & pourpointz de toile d'argent. A la queue defdicts Efcuyers eftoit l'un de fes portemanteaux, & deux huiffiers de fa chambre, parez de robbes & fayes de veloux blanc, decouppez & r'atachez de boutons d'or, portans leurs maffes.

Autour de fa perfonne fur les deux coftez, eftoyent a pié les vingtquatre Archers de la garde de fon corps, auec leurs hallebardes & hocquetons blancs, faits d'or-feurerie, à la deuife dudict Seigneur. Et à fa dextre vn peu fur le derriere, marchoit Monfeigneur de Longue-uille, grand Chambellan, & à gauche Monfeigneur le Duc de Guyfe premier Chambellan, richemét armez & veftuz, à fauoir mondict Seigneur de Longueuille, de faye de toile d'argent, enrichy de diuers compartimens, fueillages, neuz de canetille, & cordons d'or, fon cha-peau & les bardes de fon cheual de mefme.

Et módict Seigneur le Duc de Guyfe, de faye de drap d'argent, couuert de croix de Hierufalem, auec diuers fueillages & compartimens de canetille d'or, & fe r'ap-portoyét à fondict habillement fon chapeau & les bar-des de fon cheual.

Le Roy paffant en ceft ordre, pompe, & magnificen-ce, fut veu par les habitans de ladicte ville, auec vne ioye & allegreffe incroyable, ainfi que en feirent foy les ac-clamations & prieres qu'ils luy faifoyét de lieu à autre, à haulte voix, de longue vie & profperité. mefmes les eftrangers furpris d'admiration de la fingularité & richeffe

cheſſe des choſes cy deuant deſcrites, & encores beaucoup plus de la preſence d'un ſi vertueux, magnanime,
& accomply Prince, faiſoyent publiquemét confeſsion
de ſa grãdeur. Et(qui ne ſemble moins decét que louable en ſi excellent Roy)de la grace,diſpoſitió, & adreſ-
ſe qui ſe repreſentoit en ſa perſonne, auſsi perfecte que
en autre Monarque qui ayt iamais eſté.

Ledict Seigneur(oultre les autres choſes grandes &
dignes de perpetuelle memoire & recommãdation qui
furent veues en ceſte entree) fut accompagné & ſuyui
des Princes de ſon ſang, & autres Princes qui s'enſuyuent,a ſcauoir de

Mõſeigneur le Duc de Vandoſmois le premier,ayãt à
coſté de luy Loys Monſieur de Vandoſme ſon frere.

Suyuant eulx de Monſeigneur le Duc de Montpenſier ,coſtoyé par Monſeigneur le Prince de la Roche
furyon ſon frere.

Monſeigneur le Duc de Nemours eſtoit apres tenant
le milieu,à coſté de luy à main droicte, Monſeigneur le
Duc de Niuernoys , & à gauche Monſeigneur le Duc
d'Aumalle.

Monſeigneur le Marquis Dumaine venoit conſecu-
tiuement,ayant au deſſus de luy Monſeigneur le Cheualier de Lorraine, & au deſſoubs René Monſeigneur
de Lorraine ſes freres.

Les derniers furent Monſeigneur de Rohan au mi-

lieu, à cofté droit Monfeigneur le Duc d'Atrye, & à gau
che Monfeigneur le Duc de Some, qui font deux Princes eftrangers.

Tous les deffufdicts Princes (que leur grandeur &
louable vertu rend agreables & recómandez à vn chacun) eftoyent parez de harnois riches & exquiz, s'il y en
à au monde, & de fayes de draps ou toiles d'or & d'argent, couuerts de tant de fortes de compartimés, fueillages, & neuz de canetilles d'or & d'argét, chacun felon fes deuifes, que la braueté & richeffe fans l'enrichif-
fement des pierreries, perles, boutons, & fers d'or qu
eftoyent deffus , & iufques aux bardes mefmes de leur
cheuaux, eftans de la mefme parure que le demòuran
de leurfdicts habillemens, en eftoit incroyable.

A leur queue eftoit Monfieur de Canaples Cheualie
de l'ordre, Capitaine d'une des bédes des cét Gentils hò
mes de l'hoftel du Roy, et le feigneur de fainct Cire, lie
tenát de Mófeigneur le grád Efcuyer, capitaine de l'au
tre defdictes bádes, ayans à leur fuyte les deux cés gétil
hommes, auec armet en tefte, & la lance fur la cuiffe, p
rez deffus leurs harnois de fayes de veloux noir , faitz
broderie de toile d'argent, & fatin blanc, aux chiffres &
deuifes du Roy, les bardes de leurs cheuaulx de mefme

Apres eftoyét les. SS. de Chauigny, Eftrée, & la Ferte
trois Capitaines des gardes. Et quant au Seigneur d
Lorges capitaine de la garde Efcoffoife , qui euft efté l
premier, il marchoyt deuant auec les Cheualiers d
l'ordre. Lefdicts trois capitaines eftoyent habillez d
leurs hocquetons tous couuerts d'orfeurerie d'or, & a-
uoyen

uoyent fuyuant eulx leurs lieutenants, enfeignes,& les
quatre cens archers de la garde, armez comme lefdicts
deux cés gentils hommes, & eftoyent reueftuz par deffus de leurs hocquetós d'orfeurerie à la deuife du Roy.
A leur queue fuyuoyent les pages defdicts gentils hommes & archers, fuyuiz de dix archers de la garde, qui fu
rent laiffez fur le derriere pour garder qu'il n'y euft aucun defordre.

Le Roy en l'ordre, compagnie & magnificence que
deffus, entra dedans fa bonne ville & cité de Paris, capitale de fon Royaume, par la porte fainct Denis, &
chemina par la rue qui va de ladicte porte, au Chaftellet,
& dela par le Pont noftre Dame, iufques à l'Eglife noftre Dame:& par les rues(oultre le plaifir qu'il eut de la
fingularité des ouurages & deuifes qui eftoyét aux arcs
de triúphe & autres fpectacles cy deuant d'efcripts,&
de la diuerfité des inftrumés qui fonnoyét efdicts lieux
durát tout le iour de ladicte entree) il trouua lefdictes
rues tendues de riches tapifferies, les feneftres & ou-
uroers des maifons couuers de grás & beaux tappiz veluz,& rempliz d'un nombre incroyable de dames, damoifelles, bourgeoifes, gétilz hommes, officiers,& gens
d'eftoffe & apparence habitans de ladicte ville, & iufques fur les couuertures des maifons, ou partie des fpe
ctateurs, pour n'eftre les maifons capables d'une fi gráde multitude de perfónes que celle qui y eftoit, auoyét
efté contrainctz de fe retirer, fans le peuple infiny qui e-
ftoit par lefdictes rues, fi ferré, toutesfois que durát ladi
cte entrée il ne fe feift iamais aucū defordre ne cófufió.

Le Roy eftant paruenu en ladicte eglife noftre Dame

descendit pour y aller faire son oraison, ainsi qu'il est de
bóne & louable coustume, & fut suyui seulement des
Princes & Cheualiers de l'ordre qui l'accópagnerét en
ladicte eglise. Et à fin que pendant ce téps il n'entreuint
aucune cófusion, les deux cens gentils hómes, & quatre
cens archers s'arresterét sur le pót Nostre dame, iusques
à ce que le Roy fut de retour de ladicte eglise, & passé
iusques à la rue de la Caládre, pour gaigner le Palais, à
l'entrée duquel y eut deuant les gráds degrez de la pierre de marbre encores vn arc triúphal à double ouuertu
re de l'orde de Corinthe dont les collonnes furent ca-
nellées iusques à la tierce partie respódáte deuers l'em-
pietemét qui estoit toute plaine et argétée, mais par dessus reuestue de bráches de l'aurier. Sur le piedestal de
celle du milieu iaspé cóme ses collateraulx seoit vne Mi-
nerue de relief tant exquise en sa forme, que si elle eust
esté telle en Ida, le berger Phrygien n'eust adiugé la pó-
me d'or à Venus: toutesfois elle estoit vestue en deesse
digne de grande veneration. dessoubs ses pieds auoit vn
tas de liures pour dóner à entédre qu'elle est tresoriere
de sciéce: & de sa main gauche espraignoit sa mamelle
droitte dót il sortoit du laict, signifiant la doulceur qui
prouient des bónes lettres: en sa main droicte elle tenoit
des fruicts, cóme aduertissát vn chacū, que iamais biés ne
faudrót à tous ceux qui s'efforcerót de deseruir sa grace.
Ie ne vueil pas en cest édroict particularizer les mébru
res de cest arc, n'y declairer leurs enrichissemens, d'autát
que la figure est pour cela : mais bien vueil dire que sur
les bouts de la cornice estoyét seátes deux harpyes auec
chacune un flambeau en sa griffe, dont la fumée sailloit
plus odoráte que de beniouyn, ou d'oyselletz de cypre.
Dessus le sode entre ces deux harpyes y auoit deux tres
belles Nymphes vestues à l'antique, tenantes amont vn

chapeau de Laurier,pour paremét des efcuz du Roy,&
de la Royne, enuironnez l'un de fon ordre,& couróné
d'une tiaire imperiale,& l'autre d'une cordeliere fortát
de deffoubs une couronne Royale.L'une de ces Nymphes accoftant lefcu du Roy portoit vne buccine cóme
pour aduertir le móde, que du triumphe de ce puiffant
Monarque fera perpetuelle renommée par tous les cli-
mats de la mer & de la terre.Pareillemét la fuauité fortát des vafes pofezfur les extremitez du fode,alloit par-
fumer la demeure des dieux, lefquels pour retribution
donnerót infalliblemét perpetuele felicité au Roy & au
Royaume. Les flács de l'efcalier eftoyét aufsi bié garniz
de colonnes regnátes iufques au plan par ou l'on entre
en la gallerie qui meine en la grand falle, & deffus fe le-
uoit vn berfeau d'ouurage topiaire, entrelaffé & enrichy des armes auec les deuifes non feulemét de fa maiefté trefchreftienne, mais auec ce de fon efpoufe: chofe
qui donnoit grád contentemét de veue à tous ceulx qui
paffoyent par deffoubs,cóme en pareil faifoyent les feftons pendans aux coftez,& fouftenás les armoyries de
Meffeigneurs les Daulphin,& Duc d'Orleans,efperáces
de ce Royaume. Par c'eft efcalier iceluy Seigneur accópagné des Princes de fon fang, & Seigneurs deffus nómez,móta en fon Palais,qu'il trouua paré & accouftré,
non feulement de belles & riches tapifferies, mais aufsi
d'autres fingularitez infinies.La fut fait le foir en la gráde falle dudiét Palais le fouper Royal,dót l'ordre tát de
l'affiette que du feruice fut tel qui fenfuit : Sur le milieu
de la table de marbre qui eft en ladiéte grád falle fut té-
du vn doz de veloux pers,femé de fleurs de lis d'or
traiét,foubs lequel fut pofée la chaize ou s'afsift le Roy
pour fouper.A fa main droiéte Mófeigneur le Cardinal
de Bourbó, comme Prince du fang, & tenant fon reng

de leglife fut affis,& au deffoubs de luy du mefme cofté
Monfeigneur le reuerendifsime Cardinal de Védofme,
aufsi comme Prince du fang, & tenãt fon reng de legli
fe: à main feneftre dudiɛt Seigneur, Mófeigneur le Duc
de Vandofmois. Au deffoubs de luy Loys Monfieur de
Vendofme fon frere, Mófeigneur le Duc de Montpenfier apres,& Mófeigneur le Prince de la Roche furyon
fon frere, le dernier. De l'autre cofté de la table demeura debout Monfeigneur le Conneftable, lequel durant
le foupper tint fon efpée de Cóneftable nue en la main
deuant le Roy. Et quant au feruice, Monfieur le Ma-
refchal de fainɛt André feruit de grand Maiftre, au lieu
de módiɛt Seigneur le Cóneftable, Mófeigneur le Duc
de Guife de panetier, Mófeigneur de Nemours d'efchã
fon, Monfeigneur de Neuers de varlet trenchant.& fut
la viande portée par les gétils hommes de la chambre.

Au deffoubs de ladiɛte table de marbre à main droi-
ɛte tirant iufques à la porte de la falle des merciers, fut
dreffée une autre table ordonnée pour les autres Princes, Ambaffadeurs, & Cheualiers de l'ordre. De l'autre
cofté de ladiɛte falle à main gauche, depuis la chambre
du plaidoyé tirãt à la chapelle, pour la Court de Parlement, Chãbre des comptes, Generaux des aides & autres. & à l'oppofite de l'autrepart, depuis la porte dela
diɛte falle des merciers, allant cótre bas vers la porte des
petitz degrez, pour le corps de la ville.

Le Roy feiourna audiɛt Palais iufques apres l'entrée
de la Royne, l'ordre de laquelle à femblé deuoir eftre
adioufté à la fin de la prefente, pource que la plus part
des magnificences en dependent, dont la repetition ne
feroit que vne longue rediɛte.   F I N.

Sensuit l'ordre de lentree

DE LA ROYNE.

E dixhuictieme iour dudict mois de Iuin, la Royne eftant arriuée le matin au Prieuré Sainct Ladre, marcherent au deuant d'elle les quatre ordres Men-dianes, les Eglifes: les gens de pié efleuz des dixfept meftiers:les menuz officiers de ville : les archers, haquebutiers & arbaleftiers : le Preuoft des Marchans, Efcheuins, & Confeillers de la-dicte ville:le Cheualier du guet: les fergens à pié,& fie-fez : les notaires, les commiffaires, & les fergens de la douzaine:le Preuoft dudict Paris, auec fes Lieutenants: les gens du Roy, & Confeillers, & les aduocats & pro-cureurs du Chaftelet:les fergens à cheual:les generaulx des monnoyes,& des aides: Mefsieurs de la chábre des Comptes, & de la Court de Parlement, en la mefme ordonnance & parure qu'ils auoyent faict le diman-che precedant au deuant du Roy:referué ledict Preuoft de Paris, lequel eftoit en armes à l'entree dudict Sei-gneur,& fut au deuát de ladicte Dame, en robe de drap d'or frizé fur champ cramoyfi rouge, enrichy de pier-reries,& boutons d'or, monté fur vne mulle enharna-chée de harnois de veloux cramoyfi, couuert de grans & larges paffemens d'or, la houffe de mefmes: & eftoit deuant luy l'un de fes Efcuyers monté fur un braue che ual d'Efpagne richement enharnaché, & entre ledict cheual & ledict Preuoft deux de fes pages, & autát de fes lacquaiz, habillez de veloux tané, leurs accouftremés

enrichiz de broderies des couleurs dudict Preuoſt.

Les enfans de la ville qui auoyent le iour de l'entrée
du Roy chemiſes de maille , porterent ce iour là tous
pourpoints de ſatin blanc decouppé: & meſmes les aucuns d'eulx changerent d'accouſtremens,& furent habillez de ſayes de veloux blanc decouppez , & r'appor-
tez auec vne infinité de boutons,& grains d'or.

Il y eut auſſi grand nombre de ceulx des dixſept meſtiers,Imprimeurs,Sergens,& autres qui chágerét d'ac-
couſtremés,& meſmes le Preuoſt des marchás fut veſtu
ce iour là de robbe mipartie de veloux cramoyſi de
haulte couleur,& de veloux tané,l'ayant portée le iour
de l'entrée du Roy de veloux cramoyſi brun,& veloux
tané , ſon ſaye auſſi qui eſtoit ledict iour de ſatin cramoyſi, eſtoit de veloux tané figuré.

Tous les deſſuſdicts,ayans trouué ladicte Dame ſur
le meſme eſchauffault qui auparauant auoit eſté prepa-
ré pour le Roy, accópagnée de pluſieurs Princes,Prin-
ceſſes,Seigneurs, & Dames, & meſmement de Meſſeigneurs les Conneſtable , & Chancellier de France, luy
feirent la reuerence, ainſi qu'il eſt de bonne , & louable
couſtume.

Et apres luy auoir faict propoſer par les principaulx
d'entre eulx leurs harengues,ſ'en retournerét en la ville
en pareil ordre qu'ils en eſtoyent partiz.

La ville incontinent apres ſalua ladicte Dame de la
meſme quantite d'artillerie qu'elle auoit faict le Roy:&
cela faict,quelque interualle de temps apres, marcherent

rent ceulx qui eſtoyent de ſa compagnie.

Et premierement l'un des Preuoſts des Mareſchaulx
de France nommé Claude l'Hoſte, auec ſes Lieutenant
Greffier & Archers.

Apres les pages des Gentils hommes, Seigneurs &
Princes, montez ſur cheuaulx de ſeruice braues, & richement enharnachez : mais pour plus grande magnificence, d'autre parure que le iour de l'entrée du Roy.

A leur queue les Preuoſts de l'hoſtel auec leurs Lieutenás, le Procureur du Roy, leurs Greffiers, & leurs Ar
chers portans leurs hocquetons d'orfeurerie.

Et eulx paſſez, vindrent les gétilz hommes des Princes, Princeſſes, Dames, & grans Seigneurs qui accom-
pagnoyent la Royne, & ſuyuant eulx grád nombre de
Gentilz hommes, la pluſpart gentils hommes ſeruans,
& Eſcuyers d'eſcuyrie du Roy, habillez de robbes ou
ſayes de diuerſes ſortes de draps de ſoye, & differentes
couleurs, enrichiz de broderies, & boutons d'or.

Apres les Gentils hommes de la chambre, & parmi
eulx les Contes, Capitaines, & grans Seigneurs, les vns
parez de robbes de drap d'or frizé, & les autres d'autres differétes ſortes de draps d'or, d'argent, & de ſoye,
la pluſpart couuerts de pierreries, boutons, & fers d'or
tous montez ſur braues & gallans cheuaulx richement
enharnachez.

Apres eulx marcherent les Audienciers de France,
& commis du Cótrerolleur de laudience allans deuant

A ii

eulx les deux Maiſtres d'hoſtel & le ſecretaire de Monſeigneur le Chácellier, & ſuyuant leſdicts Audiencier & Contrerolleur, les Maiſtres des requeſtes de l'hoſtel du Roy veſtuz de robbes de ſatin noir, les deux huiſſiers de la chácellerie apres à pié, veſtuz de robbes de veloux cramoyſi violet, portans leurs maſſes au poing.

Monſeigneur le Chácellier les ſuyuit ſans le ſeau, habillé de robbe de toile d'or figuré ſur champ cramoiſy rouge, ſa mulle enharnachée de harnoys de veloux noir frágé d'or, la houſſe de meſme, & auoit à ſes deux coſtez quatre de ſes lacquaiz habillez de veloux noir, & apres luy ſes deux eſcuyers.

Apres vindrét les Ambaſſadeurs reſidés pres la perſonne du Roy, aſſauoir celuy de Ferrare, qui fut accomgné de Monſieur leueſque de Bayeulx.

Les trois Ambaſſadeurs de la ſeigneurie de Veniſe vindrent apres luy, ſuyuant l'autre: le premier accompagné de Monſieur l'Eueſque d'Eureux: le deuxieme, qui eſtoit habillé à la Venicienne d'une grande robbe longue de veloux cramoyſi de haulte couleur, & par deſſus d'un camail de damas cramoyſi, fermé ſur leſpaule gauche à groz boutons d'or, eſtoit accompagné de Monſieur l'Eueſque de Terouenne : & le troiſieme de Monſieur l'Eueſque de Rennes.

L'ambaſſadeur d'Eſcoſſe fut apres, accompagné de Monſieur lE'ueſque de Clermont.

A ſa queue l'Ambaſſadeur du Roy d'Angleterre, accompagné de Monſieur l'Eueſque de Montdeuis.

Suyuant

Suyuāt luy l'Ambaſſadeur de l'Empereur, accōmpa-
gné de Monſieur l'Eueſque de Chartres.

Apres l'Ambaſſadeur du Pape, le dernier, accompagné de Monſieur l'Arceueſque de Vienne Primat.

Et fault noter que tous les deſſuſdiꝰs Eueſques & Ar-
ceueſques eſtoyét reueſtuz de leurs rochets, chappes, &
chapeaux paſtoraulx.

Leſdiꝰs Ambaſſadeurs paſſez, vindrét les cent Suyſſes de la garde du Roy, & deuant eulx le filz aiſné de
Monſieur le Mareſchal de la Marche, Capitaine de ladiꝰe garde, tenant le lieu de ſondiꝰ pere, en la meſme
parure, & ordonnance qu'ils auoyent faiꝰ à l'entrée
du Roy.
Apres les phiffres, & trompettes, ſonnás de leurs in-
ſtrumens. Et à leur doz les Heraulx d'armes, reueſtuz
de leur cottes d'armes.

Apres eulx marcherent deux pages d'honneur de la
Royne, nues teſtes: le premier portant le manteau de ladiꝰe Dame, & l'autre le coffret aux bagues, habillez de
toile d'argent, & leurs cheuaulx couuerts de meſme
iuſques en terre.
Suyuāt eulx eſtoit le premier Eſcuyer de ladiꝰe Dame, habillé de veloux blanc decouppé, & r'apporté de
boutons & fers d'or, monté ſur vn cheual blanc, auſſi
couuert de toile d'argent comme les deux autres.

Le cheual de crouppe de ladiꝰe Dame venoit apres,
vn page de la meſme parure que les deux autres deſſus,

& eſtoit lediƈt cheual blanc, & tout couuert de toile
d'argent frizée trainant iuſques en terre : la houſſe & la
planchette qui eſtoit par deſſus de meſme parure.

A ſa queue la hacquenée de parade blãche, toute couuerte auſsi iuſques en terre de toile d'argent frizée: la
houſſe pardeſſus de meſme , & eſtoit menée par deux
Eſcuyers de ladiƈte Dame, habillez de robbes develoux
blãc, & ſayes de toile d'argét, & les pãs de ladiƈte houſſe portez par deux pages habillez de toile d'argent.

Cela paſſé marcherent les pages de ladiƈte Eſcuyrie
habillez de blanc & verd, qui ſont les couleurs de ladiƈte Dame, tous à pié.

Apres eulx les deux cent Gentilshommes de la maiſon du Roy, reueſtuz de robbes de diuerſes ſortes, portans chacun leurs haches en la main, & marchans à pié
deux à deux en bien bonne ordonnance.

A leur queue les Seigneurs de Boyſi & de Canaples,
leurs Capitaines, ayans leurs grans ordres au col , &
eux treſrichement parez.

Apres les laquaiz de ladiƈte Dame, tous habillez de
toile d'argent.
Monſieur le Preuoſt de Paris qui eſtoit paré cõme il
eſt diƈt, vint apres & vn peu deuãt la litiere de la Royne monté ſur ſa mule.

Monſeigneur de ſainƈt André Cheualier d'honneur
de ladiƈte Dame eſtoit ſur la main gauche de ladiƈte litiere

tiere habillé de toile d'argent,môté fur vn cheual blâc,
ayât fon harnois & la houffe de mefme parure que fon
accouftrement.

Monfeigneur le Conneftable comme grand Maiftre
de France portant en fa main le bafton de grâd Maiftre,
enrichi d'or à deuifes, eftoit fur la main droiâe plus
pres de ladiâe Dame, môté aufsi fur vn cheual d'efpa-
gne trefrichemét enharnaché, & luy habillé de robbe
de drap d'or frizé.

Suyuant luy deux huifsiers de châbre de ladiâe Dame à pié portâs leurs maffes au poing,veftuz de veloux
blanc.
La Royne venoit apres dedâs vne litiere defcouuerte,dont le fons par le dedâs & par le dehors eftoit couu-
uert de toile d'argeut trainant en terre, les mulets qui la
portoyent, tous couuerts de toile d'argent frizée auffi
trainant en terre,& les deux pages qui eftoyent deffus,
& menoyent ladiâe litiere habillez de toile d'argent les
teftes nues.

Ladiâe Dame eftoit habillée de furcot d'hermines
couuert de pierreries de grâde excellence & ineftimable valeur,de corfet & manteau Royal,portât fur fa tefte vne courône enrichie d'infinies perles & pierreries,
& auoit viz à viz delle à l'autre bout de fa litiere Madame Marguerite accouftrée & parée de furcot,corfet,&
mâteau ducal:& eftoyét les enrichiffemens tels que lon
peult penfer conuenables & feants à fi grâdes & ver-
tueufes Princeffes . Aux deux coftez de la litiere de la
Royne marchoyét quatre Cardinaux reueftuz de leurs

rochets, aſſauoir Meſſeigneurs les reuerédiſsimes Cardi
naux d'Amboiſe & de Chaſtillon les premiers, vn peu
plus auant que ladiѐte litiere. Et ſuyuant eulx aux deux
coſtez de ladiѐte Dame, Meſſeigneurs les reuerendiſsi-
mes Cardinaux de Boulongne & de Lenoncourt.

Ioignant ſadiѐte litiere eſtoyét quatre de ſes Eſcuyers
d'Eſcuyerie marchans à pié, tous habillez de robbes de
veloux blãc, & ſayes de toile d'argét, & au tour de ladiѐte Dame les vingt quatre archers de la garde du corps
du Roy, reueſtuz de leurs hocquetons blãcs, faiѐts d'orfeurerie à la deuiſe du Roy.

Au deſſus de ladiѐte Dame eſtoit vn poiſle de drap d'or
frizé, frangé de ſoye cramoyſie rouge, la creſpine de deſ
ſus de fil d'argent, aux armoiries de ladiѐte Dame, & fut
porté par ceulx meſmes qui porterent celuy du Roy.

Ladiѐte Dame eſtoit ſuyuie de Madame la Ducheſſe
Deſtouteuille Conteſſe de Sainѐt Pol, accompagnée de
Loys Monſieur de Vandoſme la premiere.

La ſeconde, Madame de Montpenſier laiſnée, accompagnée de Móſeigneur le Duc de Mótpenſier ſon filz.

La troiſieme Madame de Montpenſier la ieune, accópagnée de Móſeigneur le Príce de la Rocheſuryó.

Madame la Princeſſe de la Roche ſuryon qui eſtoit la
quatrieme, & deuoit eſtre accópagnée de Móſeigneur
de Longueuille, fut conduite par Monſeigneur le Duc
de Guyſe grãd pere de módiѐt Seigneur de Lógueuille.
Et

Et Madame la Ducheſſe de Guyſe, la cinquieme par mondiƈt Seigneur le Duc de Longueuille, en la place de mondiƈt Seigneur le Duc de Guyſe ſon grand pere.

La ſixieme fut Madame la Ducheſſe de Nyuernois la ieune, accõpagnée deMõſeigneur le Duc de Nemours.

La ſeptieme Madame d'Aumalle, accompagnée de Monſeigneur le Duc de Nyuernois.

La huiƈtieme Madame de Valentinois, accõpagnée de Monſeigneur le Duc d'Aumalle.

La neufieme Madamoiſelle la Baſtarde, accompaignée de Monſeigneur le Marquis Dumaine.

La dixieme Madame la Conneſtable, accompagnée de Monſeigneur le Cheualier de Lorraine.

Et la derniere, Madamoiſelle de Nemours, accõpagnée de René Monſieur de Lorraine.

Et fault noter que toutes leſdiƈtes Princeſſes & Dames eſtoyent montées ſur hacquenées blanches, enharnachées de toile d'argent, & elles habillées de ſurcots d'hermines, corſets, manteaux, & cercles de Ducheſſes, & Conteſſes. Les queues de leurs manteaux eſtoyent portées par leurs Eſcuyers, marchans à pié apres elles tous veſtuz de veloux ou ſatin blanc, & chacune d'elles ſuyuie de deux lacquaiz de meſme parure, ayás leſdiƈtes Dames leurſdiƈts ſurcots enrichiz de grand nombre de pierreries, reſerué les veſues qui portoyƈt leurs accou-

B

ſtremens ſans aucun enrichiſſement.

Suyuant elles marcha Madame la Mareſchale dela Marche, dame d'hóneur, treſrichement veſtue, accompagnée de Monſeigneur de Rohan.

Apres elle Madame la Mareſchale de Sainɛt André, accópagnée du Seigneur de Lorges, Cheualier de l'ordre, & l'un des Capitaines des gardes.

Madamoiſelle la baſtarde d'Eſcoſſe la troiſieme.

Madamoiſelle de Breſſures la quatrieme.

Madamoiſelle d'Auaugour la cinquieme.

La Signore Siluia, fille aiſnée du Conte de la Mirande la ſixieme.

La Signore Fuluia ſa ſeur, la ſeptieme.

La Conteſſe de Sainɛt Aignan la huiɛtieme.

Madame d'Achon la neuſieme.

Madamoiſelle de Clermont la dixieme.

Et Madamoiſelle de Humieres la derniere.

Leſdiɛtes Dames & Damoiſelles eſtoyent accompagnées de Cheualiers de l'ordre, & parées de robbes de toile d'argent enrichies d'infinies perles & pierreries, toutes mótées ſur haquenées bláches enharnachées & houſſées de meſme parure.

Les ſuſdiɛtes Dames paſſées, vindrent trois chariots branſlans l'un ſuyuant l'autre, menez chacū par quatre cheuaulx blancs enharnachez de toile d'argent, & les charretiers veſtuz de meſme parure: leſdiɛts chariots eſtoyent couuerts ſeulement par le hault de toile d'argét enrichie de houppes d'argét, & le bois rouages, limós, & tout ce qui depend deſdiɛts chariots, argenté d'argét fin. En chacun deſquels chariots eſtoyent ſix Damoiſelles

les de ladiꝰe Dame, toutes reueſtues de toile d'argent.

Suyuant leſdiꝰs chariots eſtoyent les Capitaines des gardes, auec leurs Lieutenás, enſeignes, & guidós, auec tous les Archers de la garde montez à cheual, reueſtuz de leurs hoquetons d'orfeurerie à la deuiſe du Roy.

La Royne en la pópe & magnificence que deſſus, entra dedans ladiꝰe ville de Paris, & paſſant par la porte & rue de Sainꝰ Denys, & dela par le pót noſtre Dame, qu'elle trouua en la meſme parure qu'ils eſtoyét le iour de l'entrée du Roy, vint à l'Egliſe noſtre Dame, ou elle deſcédit pour y faire ſon oraiſon, & auec elle aucús Príces, Móſeigneur le Chácelier, & quelques vns des Cheualiers de l'ordre, & des Dames, Madame Marguerite. Et pour porter la queue du manteau de la Royne Madame de Montpenſier laiſnée, Madame de Montpéſier la ieune, & Madame la Princeſſe de la Rocheſuryon.
Quant à celle de Madame Marguerite, elle fut portée par Meſsieurs de la Trimouille & de Montmorancy: & celles de mes Dames de Montpenſier laiſnée, de Montpenſier la ieune, & de la Princeſſe de la Rocheſuryon, par les Contes & grans Seigneurs ordonnez pour cela.

Ladiꝰe Dame ſon oraiſon acheuée s'en alla au Palais, ou à la deſcéte la queue de ſon máteau luy fut auſsi portée par mes Dames de Vandoſme, de Sainꝰ Pol, & de Montpenſier laiſnée: & celles des manteaux deſdiꝰes Dames par Contes, & autres grans Seigneurs deputez pour ce faire.
Le ſeoir fut fait le ſoupper Royal auec les cerimonies & ſolennitez cy deſcriptes.

B ii

Ladicte Dame qui fut afsife au mefme lieu que auoit efté le Roy le iour de fon entrée, & foubs vn doz de veloux pers, femé de fleurs de lis d'or, auoit afsis à fa main droicte Monfeigneur le reuerendifsime Cardinal de Chaftillon,& au deffoubs de luy les Ambaffadeurs cy deuant nómez en leur ordre. A fa main gauche mes Dames de Vandofme, de Sainct Pol, de Montpenfier lainée, de Montpenfier la ieune,Princeffe de la Roche furyó,de Guyfe,de Neuers laifnée,& de Neuers la ieune,d'Aumalle,& de Valentinois, Madamoifelle la baftarde, Madame la Conneftable, Madamoifelle de Nemours,& Madame la Marquife Dumaine.

Mófeigneur le Conneftable feruit audict foupper de grand Maiftre,Loys Mófieur de Vádofme de panetier, Monfeigneur de Montpenfier d'efchanfon, & Monfeigneur le Prince de la Rochefuryon d'efcuyer trenchát & porterent la viande les Gentils hommes de la chambre du Roy.

Quant aux autres tables elles furent ordonnées cóme le iour de l'entrée dudict Seigneur, & fans autre difference, finon que celle qui feruit à ladicte entrée pour aucūs des Princes,& les Cheualiers de l'ordre,fut pour les autres Dames & Damoyfelles qui auoyent tenu rág à ladicte entrée.

Le lendemain ladicte Dame alla oyr la meffe en l'Eglife Noftre dame de Paris, ou le Preuoft des marchás accópagné des Efcheuins, Greffier,Confeillers,& plufieurs des enfans de la ville,la vindrent treshumblemét fupplier, que fó bó plaifir feuft leur faire cefte grace de prédre

prédre fa refeƈtió en vne gráde fale de la maifon de Mõ
feigneur le reuerédifsime Cardinal du Bellay,qui eftoit
pour elle appareillée.ce que ladiƈte Dame liberalement
accorda:& pour ce faire móta par vn efcalier beau & ri
che à merueilles, cómenceát des l'yffue de la porte d'i-
celle eglife, & regnát cóme vn pont iufques au logis de
mondiƈt Seigneur le Cardinal. Ou eftant arriuée,fa ma
iefté auec plufieurs Princeffes, Dames & Gentils hommes fe prindrent à contempler la beaulté de ladiƈte fale,pour les belles painƈtures dont elle eftoit noblement
decorée. C'eftoyent les figures des dieux & deeffes qui
fe trouuerent aux nopces de Peleus & Tethis, pere &
mere du grand Achilles . Entre ces figures colloquées
foubs le rabbat fur quoy pofe la couuerture de la fale,
faiƈte en hemicycle, eftoyent de fingulierement beaux
paifages,tant bien reprefentás le naturel, que ceulx qui
les regardoyent, & auec ce les geftes de plufieurs perfonnages s'esbatans à tous les ieux aufquels la venerable
ble antiquité fe fouloit auec pris exerciter,perdirét l'ap
petit de boire & de menger.

Ie ne m'occupe point apres les compartimés migno-
tez de grotefques,dont ces pieces eftoyét bordées,mais
tant y a qu'encores que Vitruue & Horace les ayét de-
teftées,leur inuention fe monftroit fi plaifante , qu'on
n'en pouoit ofter la veue.

Deffoubs cela pédoit iufques à terre vne riche tapifferie de haulte liffe,pareillemét à perfonnages,qu'il faifoit merueilleufement bon veoir, & enuironnoit tous
les quatre flács de la fale,qui s'en pouoyent tenir à bien
parez.

Sur ce rabat feoit vn lacunaire, ou plancher plat, à parquets de morefques, dorées & diuerfifiées de maintes couleurs, foubs rofaces d'or, embouties tant au milieu que fur les quatre coings, qui (veritablement) donnoyent vn grád efclat, ioint que cefdiĉts parquets à l'endroit de leurs commiffures, eftoyent garniz de feftons de lyerre, dont la verdeur ne pouuoit finon rédre plaifir & deleĉtation.

Tel eftoit l'ornement de la falle preparée pour ladiĉte Dame, laquelle quand bon luy fembla, print l'eau pour lauer, & puis fe meit à table auec les Princeffes du fang: ou fa maiefté fut feruie de toutes les viádes exquifes que produifoit nature en la faifon. Et tint le Preuoft des marchans pour ce iour le lieu de fon Maiftre d'hoftel, eftant fuyui à l'afsiette des plats, par les Gétilshómes & officiers de la maifon d'icelle Dame: qui fe trouua grádement fatisfaiĉte du bó deuoir qu'il feit en la feruant.

Quant aux Dames tant de fa fuytte, que de Paris, elles s'afsirent toutes à d'autres tables expreffement pour ce dreffées du lóg des murailles de la fale: & furent feruies par les Efcheuins, Greffier, & principaulx officiers d'icelle ville, ayans apres eulx pour porter les viandes, les enfans des bónes maifons, veftuz de leurs riches habits qu'ils auoyent portez à l'entrée: parquoy c'eftoit vne droitte merueille, à raifon que les perles & pierreries, dont leurdiĉts accouftreméts eftoyét femez, brilloyent au foleil paffant atrauers les verrieres, de telle forte que la lueur reflechiffoit iufques aux Princeffes & Dames, aufsi parées de Rubis, Dyamans, Efmeraudes, & autres eftoiles terreftres, de valeur ineftimable, dont les rayós efclattás iufques au brillemét des precedétes, formoyét

en

en s'entrerencontrant, cóme vne Iris ou arc en ciel, de
forte que l'air agité par cela, mefmes par les trompettes,
clairons, & autres inftrumens de mufique, fonans me-
lodieufement à l'afsiette de tous les mets & entremets,
n'eftoit pas moins plaifant en cefte falle, qu'on l'eftime
eftre aux Ifles fortunées.

Certainement l'abondance & delicateffe des vins &
des viandes ne pourroit eftre bien à droit exprimée, &
aufsi ne feroit ce que fuperfluité, à raifon de quoy ie
m'en tay, pour dire que le bon plaifir du Roy fut d'afsi-
fter en perfonne à ce feftin, & auoir le paffetéps du bal
apres difner, cóme il eut, aufsi toft que les tables furét le-
uées, & par efpecial des enfans de la ville, lefquels au có
mandement de fa maiefté, menerent dancer les Dames
de la Court, & s'en acquitterent de bonne grace, chofe
qui contenta grandemét fadicte maiefté, enfemble tous
les Princes & Seigneurs qui fe trouuerét à cefte affem-
blée. Puis ledict bal fini, l'on redreffa nouuelles tables
au milieu de la falle, & deffus fut appporté e la collatió
de tant de fortes de dragées & autres cófitures, que l'on
ne fcauoit aufquelles fe prendre, pource que toutes e-
ftoyent exquifes chacune en fon endroict.

Cela faict le fufdict Preuoft des marchans auec les
Efcheuins de la ville, feit prefent à la Royne d'un buffet bié accópli de vaifelle d'argét doré à deux couches,
fi qu'il fembloit que ce fuft tout fin or, femé de fleurs
de lis, auec croiffans. Et fut ce prefent trouué tant
beau & riche, mefmement par ladicte Dame, qu'elle feit
demóftratió de l'auoir en eftime: mais encores print elle autant & plus à gré la harengue que luy feit à ce
propos le Preuoft des marchás, qu'elle iugea finguliere

& modeſte en ſa brieueté,par la reſponſe meſme rédue
de ſa bouche.

Le l'endemain iour de la feſte Dieu, iceluy Preuoſt
des marchás auec les Eſcheuins,Greffier, & principaux
officiers de la ville,allerét aux Tournelles preſenter au
Roy le riche preſent qu'ils auoyét faiƈt faire pour ſa ma
ieſté.Et pour donner à entendre ſa façon,Premieremét
conuient noter qu'il eſtoit tout de fin or de ducat,cize-
lé,buriné,& conduiƈt par tel artifice d'orfeurerie, que
lon ne veit oncques plus belle piece d'ouurage en toute Europe. C'eſtoit vne baſe triangulaire ſouſtenue par
trois Harpyes,aſsiſes ſur vn plan bien taillé,enrichy des
armes,deuiſes, & chiffres de ſa maieſté, meſmes bordé
de moulures exquiſes,bien à la haulteur d'un bó poul-
ce,dedás la platte báde deſquelles eſtoit eſcrit,
HENRICO II.PRINCIPI P. F. PRIN-
CEPS CIVITAS LVTETIA D. D.

La ſuperficie de celle baſe eſtoit faiƈte en terraſſe, ſemée d'herbes & de fleurettes : au milieu de laquelle
ſourdoit vn beau Palmier,le mieux contrefaiſant le naturel qu'il eſt poſsible.auſsi auoit il (certes) eſté curieu-
ment eſmaillé apres des branches veritables,apportées
d'Italie & d'ailleurs.Mais combien que les Italiénes ne
portent point de fruiƈt, ſi eſt ce nonobſtant , que l'ouurier entendu ne laiſſa point à decorer ſon arbre de ſes
grappes repreſentátes à peu pres les raiſins, qui luy dó-
noyent merueilleuſemét bonne grace. Autour de la tige de ce Palmier eſcaillée comme il appartient, eſtoyét
trois Roys plantez de bout, armez à l'antique, & reueſtuz de leurs togues imperiales, portans couronnes ſur
leurs

leurs teftes, les deux garnies de picquans, non de fleurons,mais feulemét la tierce, pour dôner à entédre que
les deux auoyent regné, & que le tiers eft de prefent en
regne.Le vifage du premier fe rapportoit nayuemét au
Roy Loys douzieme,ayeul, & celuy du fecond au Roy
Frácois,pere du triúphant, lequel aufsi pouuoit y veoir
le fien exprimé côme en vn miroer.Ces deux luy monftroyent chacun d'une main leuée vers le houppeau de
l'arbre,vne table quarrée en maniere de Cartoche, at-
tachée à l'une des branches,auec vne petite chaifnette
d'or de fubtile manifacture, dedans laquelle eftoit efcrit d'efmail blanc fur fons noir,MAGNVM MA-
GNA DECENT. Côtre les angles ou areftes de
la fufdicte bafe,eftoyent afsiz trois autres perfonnages
reprefentás l'un Ianus à deux vifages, le premier vieil,
le fecond ieune , fignifiant le temps pafsé, & le prefent.
De fa main gauche il tenoit vne table toute blanche, &
en la droicte vn greffe ou ftile pour efcrire les occurré-
ces qui fe prefenteront à l'auenir.Ceftuy la eftoit droit-
tement deffoubs le Roy Loys,pour declarer fa grád fa-
geffe & prouidence,par laquelle il merita d'eftre appel-
lé Pere du peuple. Le fecond perfonnage eftoit vne Iuftice tenát lefpée nue en la main,& foubs fes pieds la for
me d'une bourfe,pour dôner à cognoiftre que le Prince dominateur, ne veult que par pecune foyét aucune-
mét corrópuz ceulx qu'il à conftituez pour faire droit
à fes fubgects. Cefte la eftoit deffoubs le Roy Francois,
lequel par fa doulce equité à fceu gaigner le tiltre de
Prince clement en iuftice,& auec ce de reftaurateur des
bons arts & fciences, comme deffus à efté dict. Le tiers
perfonnage eftoit vn Mauors,armé à l'heroique,tenant
la main droicte fur le manche de fon efpée, & du bras

C

gauche embraſſant vne Targue à vne teſte de Lyon, pour denoter la Nobleſſe Francoiſe, touſiours appareillée à offendre ou deffendre contre les ennemis de la couronne, quand les occaſions s'en offrent . Ceſtuy la eſtoit ſoubs les pieds du Roy Henry ſecód, que Dieu maintienne en augmentation de perfecte proſperité. & à bon droict y eſtoit mis, pource que veritablemé t c'eſt le pere des Nobles, & qui d'orenauát ſera ainſi nommé tant que le monde ſera monde . Ces trois auoyent les pieds ſur les doz des Harpyes, qui repreſentét vices, cóme pour dire que par vertuz les vices doyuét eſtre exterminez. En toutes les trois faces de la baſe, y auoit les armes de France enrichies du collier de l'ordre, & courónées de couronne imperiale. Puis à l'entour du fons de lampe eſtát deſſoubs ladicte baſe, faict en facon d'une roſace , artiſtemét cizelée s'il en fut oncques, eſtoyét les armes de la ville enuironnées d'un rouleau portant ce mot, TVMIDIS VELIS, AQVILONE SECVNDO.

Voyla en ſomme quel eſtoit le preſent qui fut faict à ſa maieſté : laquelle (certes) le receut de bon cueur, cóme euidentement manifeſta la veue, qui donnoit ſigne de lieſſe pendant que la bouche royale reſpondoit à la petite harangue du ſuſdict Preuoſt des marchans, tát bien priſe que mieulx ne pouuoit eſtre, ſingulierement pour auoir expoſé l'intention de la manifacture, qui rememo roit les vertuz des deux monarques de la Gaule, & leur enſeignement vtile pour faire d'un Roy de France, vn ſeul Seigneur de tout le monde.

La reſponſe donc acheuée iceluy Preuoſt des marchans

chans fupplia treshumblement fa maiefté,que fon bon
plaifir fuſt de fe trouuer le dimenche prochain iour de
la vigile fainet Iehan Baptifte,(fuyuant l’ancienne couftume de fes predeceffeurs) en la place de greue, deuant
l’hoftel de la ville,pour la mettre le feu à vne pyramide,
ou bié châtier de boys,excefsif en haulteur,qui fe dref-
fe annuellement à tel iour, pour folennizer la memoire
de la natiuité du precurfeur de IefuChrift. ce que fa di-
ete maiefté trefchreftienne liberalement ottroya, & y
veint à l’heure dicte,accópagné de la Royne, enfemble
des Princes & Princeffes du fang, Cardinaulx,& autre
multitude venerable des plus grans Seigneurs, Dames
& Damoyfelles de fon Royaume. Adóc le Preuoft des
marchás auec les Efcheuins & Officiers de la ville fuyuiz de leurs Archers, Haquebutiers, Arbaleftiers, tró-
pettes,clairons,haulzboys,phiffres & tabourins, luy allerent au deuant en fort bon & bel ordre: & fut prefentée audiet Seigneur Roy, par iceluy Preuoft des marchans, en grande humilité , honneur & reuerence, vne
torche de cire blanche,allumée pour l’effect que deffus.
laquelle fa maiefté print, & en alluma toft apres la py-
ramide.dont fortit incontinent vne tempefte d’artillerie
entremeflée de fuzées,grenades , & autres artifices de
feu,en telle forte que le peuple circonftant demouroit
eftonné par admirable delectation: car il fembloit que
cela contrefeit Iupiter quand il voulut fouldroyer les
Geans en la campagne de Phlegra.

Ce pendant que le boys ardoit,le Roy,les Princes,les
Princeffes, les Seigneurs & les Dames de leur fuitte,
monterent en la falle haulte de l’hoftel de la ville, ou la
collation eftoit fumptueufemét appreftée,de toutes les
C ii

fortes de cõfitures,dragées,pieces de four,fruicts,& autres nouuelletez qu'on euſt ſceu trouuer pour le tẽps:
de quoy leurs maieſtez gouſterent vn petit: puis le reſte
des afsiſtans de la Court, & des bonnes maiſons de la
ville,en print ce que bon luy ſembla . dont iceulx Seigneurs & Dames ne receurent moindre contentement
que des autres magnificences parauant faictes à leurs
entrées.apres monterent à cheual, & s'en retournerent
au logis des Tournelles,aſſouuiz d'incroyable plaiſir,de
veoir le peuple de Paris tant humblement affectionné
au ſeruice de leurs maieſtez ſacrées.

Le Roy & la Royne ſeiournerent vn mois en leur
maiſon des Tournelles,& ce pédant ce feirét en la grãd
rue Sainct Anthoine pluſieurs iouſtes & tournoys. Et
fault entédre qu'aſſez pres de la voye par ou lõ tourne à
l'egliſe ſainct Pol,Meſsieurs de la ville auoyét faict faire vn bel Arc triumphal,en maniere d' H, dont les colonnes qui ſeruoyent de iãbages, furét de la facon Dorique,toutes reueſtues de trophées ou deſpouilles antiques,portant chacune trois pieds & vn quart de diametre,deſſoubs vingt & quatre de haulteur, auec leurs
baſes & chapiteaux, garniz de moulures conuenables,
ſi ſongneuſement obſeruées, que la meſure meſme
n'euſt ſceu eſtre plus iuſte . Ces colonnes eſtoyent afsi-
ſes deſſus deux piedeſtalz de dix pieds en haulteur, &
de neuf pieds d'eſpois,faiſans la profondeur de l'Arc,&
ſeruans de coſtez ou flancheres à l'ouuerture de la grãd
porte,ayant douze bons pieds de large,par ou l'on entroit dans la liſſe,dont le linteau conſtitué au lieu tra-
uerſant de l'H,fut en maniere de cornice, ſur quoy po-
ſoyent deux Victoires de relief, belles & veſtues en
vrayes

vrayes Nymphes, tenãt chacune fa palme d'une part,&
fouftenant de lautre vn grand Croiffant d'argent,d'enuiron huit pieds de diametre,pofé contre vn fons noir,
entre les cornes duquel eftoyët les armes de fa maiefté,
richement eftoffées,& garnies du tout ce qu'il y appar-
tenoit . Deffus les chapiteaux de ces colonnes y auoit
deux grans Plinthes quarrez,oultrepaffans la circunference du tailloer,de plus d'un grand pié en tous fens:&
la deffus eftoyent à cheual vn Belgius & vn Brennus,de
fi belle fculpture , que les antiques mefmes fe feuffent
contentez d'auoir faiƈt aufsi bien. leurs noms eftoyent
efcrits côtre la face du quarré qui regardoit deuers les
liffes, de quatre vingts neuf toifes d'eftédue,fur huit &
demie de large,du cofté de fainƈt Pol,mais de douze en
celuy des Tournelles,& dans chacũ de ftylobates, s'appliqua vne table ou fut efcrit,a fcauoir foubs le Belgius,
GALLO TOTIVS ASIAE VICTORI,
MEMORES NEPOTES.& en l'autre de Bré-
nus, EVROPAE DOMINORVM GAL-
LO DOMITORI, VINDICES GAL-
LI TROPHAEVM EREXERE.
Droit au milieu du plat fons du linteau, faifant le deffus de la porte,y auoit vne Cartoche antique, dedãs laquelle fe lifoit tel quatrin.

Les phalanges de Grece,& legions Romaines,
Ployerent foubs le faix de noz puiffans effors:
Sire,aufsi ployeront les plus fins & plus fors,
Deffoubs voftre prudéce & force plus qu'humaines.

A la premiere face de c'eft arc regardãt vers Sainƈte

Catherine du val des Escolliers, sur la saillie des piedestalz,estoyent vn Mauors portant pour son mot,
MARS GALLORVM DEVS,& vn Dis,qui
disoit,DIS GALLORVM PATER, si bien
ouurez, que leurs contenances incitoyent à bié faire les
hommes d'armes arriuans au tournoy, ioinct aussi que
sur le claueau de la grand porte, par dessoubs lequel ils
passoyent la lance sur la cuisse,deux Victoires toutes pa
reilles aux precedentes, faisoyent desirer à chacun renommée en cheualerie.

Aux costez d'icelle H,y auoit deux eschauffaulx, chacun de quatre toises en longueur , & de trois en haulteur,ou estoyét Messieurs de la ville pour veoir les iou-
stes à leur aise.& dessoubs eulx estoyent deux porte-
reaux par ou le peuple pouuoit passer.Mais à main gau
che deuant le milieu des lisses regnoit cestuy la de la
Royne & des Dames, lequel auoit dixhuit toises de
long,& neuf pieds en largeur, garny d'une restrainête à
deux estages,portant six toises de mesure,& vingt pieds
en haulteur : dessus laquelle estoit vn sode d'enuiron
quatre pieds de montée, enrichy d'architraue, frizé &
cornicé:mais pour l'amortissement du dessus, il y auoit
vne H,appuyée de deux K K,& ennoblie d'un croissant
au milieu,droittemét posant sur sa barre.Deux semblables estoyent à costé des arboutás,y appliquez pour en-
forcir l'ouurage:mais pour la commodité il y auoit vn
escallier seruant à monter de l'estage de bas à cestuy la
de hault: & du mesme costé regnoit vn pont de xiiii.
toises en longueur, dessus huit pieds de large,venát du
logis d'Angoulesme iusques audict eschauffault de la
Royne.

Au

Au flanc de la main droitte,côtre la maiſon commu-
nement appellée le beau treilliz,fut baſty vn autre eſchauffault de treze toiſes en longueur,ſur neuf de large,portant vingt pieds de hault,ordonné pour le Gouuerneur de Paris, enſemble pour Meſſeigneurs les Iuges du Tournoy , auec les Ambaſſadeurs deſſus nommez. mais ſur le deuát à l'endroit ou eſtoyét les iuges,y
auoit vne autre eſchauffault pour les Heraulx d'armes,
contenát quatre toiſes de long ſur quatre pieds de large en ſaillie.

Plus au bout du camp vers la premiere entrée,y auoit
vne barriere ou ſe rengeoint les hommes d'armes,& à
coſté vn petit eſchauffault , ou eſtoit vn Herault,lequel
appelloit les iouſteurs pour aller faire leur deuoir.

Mais pource que le tout ne ſe pourroit exprimer en
painĉure,que ce ne feuſt par trop gráde curioſité,vous
aurez icy leĉeurs ſeulement le deſſeing de ceſte porte.

Au trauers de la rue depuis le coing des Tournelles,
s'eſtendoit vne merueilleuſe Arcade, faiƈte par le com-
mandement & ordonnance de la maieſté du Roy,en ſi
extreme perfeƈtion de beaulté, qu'il n'eſt poſsible (ſans
ennuyer les deſirans de veoir)d'en ſpecifier les particu-
laritez:par quoy ie les remets au iugement que la veue
en pourra faire,apres auoir mis l'œil ſur le pourtraiƈt.
Mais en paſſant ie diray(toutesfois)que pardeſſus la circunference de trois portes dont elle eſtoit accommo-
dée,a ſcauoir d'une gráde au milieu, & deux moindres
à ſes coſtez,eſtoit erigée vne gráde ſalle à la mode Frá-
coiſe,garnie de croiſées à vitres, choſe ſi treſſuperbe &
excellente, qu'on la pouuoit à bon droiƈt appeller vray
ouurage de Roy,& ce teſmoignera ſon vmbre icy pre-
ſente.

F I N.

D

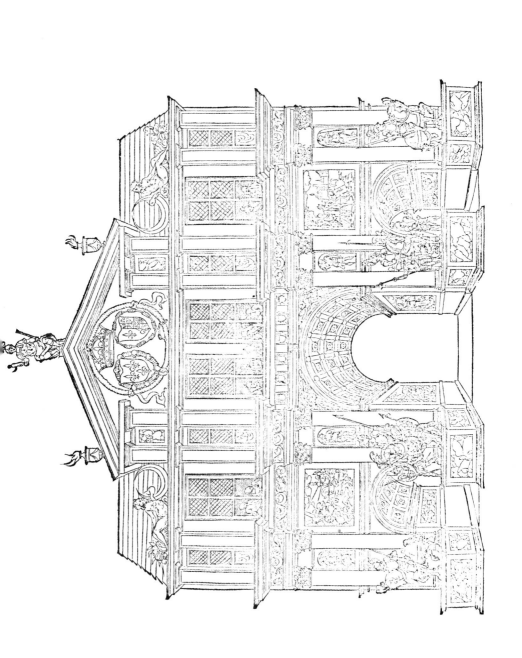

C'EST L'ORDRE

ET FORME QVI A ESTE TE-
nue au Sacre & Couronnement de treshaulte & tref-
illuftre Dame Madame Catharine de Medicis, Royne de France, faict en l'Eglife Monfeigueur fainct Denys en France, Le X. iour de Iuin.

M. D. XLIX.

A PARIS,

Par Iean Dallier Libraire, demourant fur le pont fainct
Michel à l'enfeigne de la Rofe Blanche.

PAR PRIVILEGE DV ROY.

C'EST L'ORDRE

ET FORME QVI A ESTE TE-nue au Sacre & Couronnement de treshaulte & treſilluſtre Dame Madame Catharine de Medicis, Royne de France, faict en l'Egliſe Monſeigneur ſainct Denys en France, Le X. iour de Iuin.

M. D. XLIX.

ET PREMIEREMENT pour l'acte & ſolennité dudict Sacre fut dreſſé au cueur de l'Egliſe ſainct Denys, vn grand eſchauffault poſé droict deuãt le grand autel d'icelle, de la haulteur de neuf pieds & demy ou enuiron, ayãt de lõgueur vingt & deux pieds, ſur dixneuf de large: auquel eſchauffault qui eſtoit garny de barrieres de toutes parts, l'on mõtoit du coſté dudict grand autel, dixſept marches en haulteur, & puis ſe trouuoit vne eſpace d'enuiron ſix pieds de lõg, & de largeur de ladicte mõtée, de laquelle on montoit deux autres marches pour entrer audict grand eſchauffault. Enuiron le milieu dudict eſchauffault en tirant vn peu ſur le derriere, y auoit aſſis vn hauldez de la haulteur d'vn pied ou plus, où l'on mõtoit deux marches, lequel hauldez & marches qui contenoyent de dix à vnze pieds de long, & ſix de large, eſtoyent couuerts d'vn grand drap de pied de drap d'or frizé, ſur lequel fut poſée la chaize ordonnée pour aſſeoir ladicte Dame, couuerte de veloux pers ſemé de fleurs de lys d'or, & au deſſus vn hauldez de ſemblable parure. Les coſtez des barrieres au dedans dudict eſchauffault eſtoyent tenduz de deux lez de drap d'or frizé : & par le dehors de toile d'or & d'argent, tombant à vn pied & demy de terre. Le fons & marches dudict efchauffault planchées de veloux cramoyfi, femé de broderie d'or, à K & A : & les barrieres & coftez defdictes marches, couuerts de drap d'or frizé. A main droicte dudict hauldez y auoit vne chaize couuerte de drap d'or frizé, ordonnée pour madame Marguerite fœur du Roy : & à vn pied pres de ladicte chaize vne longue felle couuerte de mefme, pour y affeoir madame la Ducheffe d'Eftouteuille, Comteffe de fainct Pol, mes dames les Ducheffes de Montpenfier, la ieune de Niuernois, la ieune d'Aumalle, & de Valentinois, madame la Conneftable, & madame la Marquife du Maine.

De l'autre cofté dudict hauldez, à main gauche, y auoit vne pareille felle couuerte de femblable parure, pour y affeoir madame la Ducheffe doüairiere de Vendofmois, madame la Ducheffe de Montpenfier l'aifnée, madame la Princeffe de la Roche fur-Yon, madame la Ducheffe de Guyfe, madamoifelle la Baftarde, & madamoifelle de Nemours.

Deuant ledict hauldez, vn peu à gauche, y auoit vn petit efcabeau couuert auffi de veloux pers femé de fleurs de lys d'or, & vn carreau de mefme parure, ordonué pour affeoir la grande Couronne, apres qu'elle feroit oftée de deffus le chef de la Royne, & qu'on luy auroit baillé la petite.

A l'entrée dudict efchauffault, au deffus & du mefme cofté dudict petit efcabeau, y en auoit vn autre, couuert

uert de drap d'or frizé, pour asseoir la Dame d'honneur de la Royne, qui est madame la Mareschalle de la Marche.

Ioignant ledict grand eschauffault, y auoit quatre eschauffaulx separez, de la mesme haulteur à peu pres que le grand, sçauoir est deux à la main droicte, dont le premier qui estoit plus petit, & plus approchant du grand autel, estoit ordonné pour asseoir les Princes : & l'autre qui estoit apres approchant ledict grand eschauffault, estoit pour les Cheualiers de l'ordre : & derriere eux, pour les gentils-hommes de la chambre, & autres grans seigneurs, capitaines, & gens d'apparence.

A la main gauche estoyent les deux autres eschauffaulx, de mesme façon, haulteur, lógueur, & largeur que les dessusdicts. Le premier correspondát à celuy desdicts Princes, estoit pour les Ambassadeurs : & l'autre correspondant à celuy desdicts Cheualiers de l'ordre, pour les Dames & Damoiselles de la Royne.

Les barrieres desdicts quatre eschauffaulx, estoyent couuertes de drap d'or frizé, faict à quilles, dudict drap d'or frizé, & de veloux cramoysi violet, semé de fleurs de lys d'or, tombát à pied & demy de terre, reserué à leschauffault desdicts Princes, où ledict drap d'or fut troussé plus hault pour donner veüe à vn petit eschauffault qui estoit dressé dessoubs, pour les Capitaines des gardes. Et estoyent lesdicts eschauffault planchées de grans tapiz de Turquie : & les bancs qui estoyent au dedans pour asseoir les assistans, couuerts les vns de toile d'or, & les autres de toile d'or & d'argent.

A la main gauche, & tenãt à la defcente dudict grand efchauffault, y auoit vn autre petit efchauffault, ordóné pour les dames, qui auoyent à bailler à ladicte dame d'honneur le pain, le vin, & le cierge, auec l'argent pour l'offerte, pour apres les bailler par ladicte dame d'honneur, aux Princeffes, & aux dames ordonnées pour les prefenter à la Royne. Lequel efchauffault eftoit tendu & planchée de veloux cramoyfi, femé de broderie d'or à K K, & à A A courónez, & le banc pour feoir lefdictes dames, couuert de drap d'or.

Du mefme cofté au bas de l'efchauffault defdicts Ambaffadeurs, & tenant à iceluy, y auoit vn banc couuert de drap d'or, pour Meffeigneurs les Cardinaulx, où furét affis Meffeigneurs les Cardinaulx de Boulógne, de Guyfe, de Chaftillon, & de Vandofme, & au bas d'iceluy vne marche l'arge d'enuiron deux pieds, couuerte de tapiz veluz, pour feoir leurs caudataires.

Plus auant au mefme cofté, affez pres du grand autel, y auoit vn autre petit efchauffault, efleué de trois à quatre pieds, pour les chantres de la chappelle du Roy, tendu par le dehors de grans tapiz veluz.

Ioignant ledict autel de ce mefme cofté, y auoit vne table hónorablement preparée, pour y pofer les Sceptre, Main de iuftice, les grandes & petites Couronnes, auec l'Anneau ordonné pour ledict facre.

De l'autre cofté à main droicte, y auoit vne chaize couuerte de drap d'or frizé, auec deux oreilliers de mefme

me parure,pour feoir mófeigneur le Cardinal de Bourbon, faifant l'office.

Des deux coftez dudiſt grand autel,y auoit des bácz
couuerts de toiles d'or & d'argent, pour les Prelats efta-
bliz tant pour feruir au facre, couronnement, & à la
meffe,que pour y affifter.

Le parterre du cueur,depuis lediſt grand efchauffault
de la Royne iufques audiſt grand autel,eftoit tout couuert de grans & richès tapiz veluz, & à l'entrée dudiſt
grand autel , par deffus lefdiſts tapiz d'vn drap de pié de
drap d'or frizé.

Hors le cueur de ladiſte Eglife,& ioignant la cloftu-
re d'iceluy, entredeux piliers , y auoit de chacun cofté
vn efchauffault en forme de theatre à cinq marches,tou
tes couuertes de riches tapifferies, pour y mettre en l'vn
qui eftoit à main gauche plufieurs dames & damoifelles,& à l'autre qui eftoit à main droiſte plufieurs gentils
hommes & gens d'apparence.

Oultre tous les deffufdiſts efchauffaulx,il en fut faiſt
vn vis à vis dudiſt grand autel, à main droiſte, plus efleué que les autres, qui fut couuert, & les feneftres bou-
chées de cages d'ozier, auquel on entroit par vne montée qui fut dreffée du cofté des corps fainſts,& eftoit lediſt efchauffault par le dedans tapiffé de riche tapifferie : les feparations & meneaux par le dehors de toile
d'argent, & le bas de veloux cramoifi, faiſt à broderie
d'or à K & A couronnez trainant iufques en terre, &

seruit ledict eschauffault au Roy pour veoir ledict couronnement, sans qu'il peust estre veu du dehors.

Ledict dixiesme iour de Iuin, lendemain de Pente-
couste, la Royne qui estoit arriuée trois iours au parauant en ladicte ville de sainct Denys, se trouua le matin
en sa chambre, habillée de corset, surcot d'hermines, mãteau, ornement de teste, & autres habits Royaux, & e-
stoit son manteau de veloux pers semé de fleurs de lis,
d'or, fourré d'hermines.

Son ornement de teste tout garny de pierreries : son-
dict corset aussi de veloux pers, couuert de fleurs de liz
d'or traict, & son surcot garny & enrichy de groz dyamans, rubiz, & emeraudes, le tout de telle excellence
& valeur, que le pris en est inestimable.

Enuiron les vnze heures du matin, messeigneurs les
reuerendissimes Cardinaux de Guyse & de Vandosme,
partirẽt de l'Eglise dudict sainct Denys, & allerent trouuer ladicte Dame, qui estoit accompaignée des Princes.
Princesses, & Dames, cy apres nommées, & de plusieurs
autres grans seigneurs, capitaines, gentils-hommes, &
dames en grande & honorable compagnie.

Les dessusdicts Cardinaux reuestuz de leurs grandes
chappes, amenerent la Royne, partant de sadicte chambre iusques à la porte de l'Eglise en l'ordre qui sensuit.

Premierement marchoyent les deux cens gẽtils-hom-
mes de la maison du Roy, les chambellans, gẽtils-hom-
mes

mes de la chambre, & parmy eux les Capitaines & autres groz personnages, qui se trouuerent audict sacre &
couronnement.

Suyuant eux les Cheualiers de l'Ordre, ayans leur
grand ordre au col.

Apres les trompettes, & les heraux, reuestuz de leurs
cottes d'armes.

A leur doz deux Huissiers de chambre portans leurs
masses.

Et apres Messeigneurs les Princes.

Puis la Royne menée & côduicte par lesdicts Cardinaux de Guyse, & de Vandosme, messeigneurs les Duc
de Vandosmois & Côte d'Anguyé, tenãs les pans de son
manteau Royal, mondict Seigneur le Duc de Vandosmois à la main droicte, & môdict Seigneur d'Anguyen
à la gauche. Marchoit apres les Princes deuant ladicte
Dame monseigneur de Montmorency Connestable &
Grandmaistre de France, auec son baston de Grandmaistre, enrichy d'or à deuises.

Mes Dames les Duchesses de Montpensier l'aisnée,
& la ieune, & madame la Princesse de la Roche-Suryon porterent la queüe du manteau de ladicte Dame.
Et celles desdictes dames furent portées, sçauoir est
celle de madicte Dame la Duchesse de Montpensier
laisnée, par monseigneur le Comte de Roussy, celle de
madicte Dame de Montpensier la ieune par monseigneur le Vidame de Chartres, & celle de madicte Dame
la Princesse par monseigneur le Conte de Villars.

B

Apres la Royne marcha madame Marguerite ſeur du Roy, ſeule, & fut la queüe de ſon manteau portée par Meſſeigneurs de la Trimoüille & de Montmorécy.

Suyuant elle meſdames les Ducheſſe doüairiere de Vandoſmois, & d'Eſtouteuille, Conteſſe de ſainctPol, l'vne quant & l'autre, tenant à la main droicte madicte Dame la Ducheſſe doüairiere de Vādoſmois, & eſtoyét les queües de leurs manteaux portées, à ſçauoir de madicte Dame la Ducheſſe doüairiere de Vandoſmois,par monſeigneur le Conte de la Chambre, & de madame d'Eſtouteuille par monſeigneur le Marquis de Neſle.

Mes Dames les Ducheſſes de Guyſe & de Niuernoys la ieune ſuiuoyent apres, & portoyent les queües de leurs manteaux, à ſçauoir de madicte Dame de Guyſe, monſeigneur de la Rochefoucault, & de madame de Niuernois monſeigneur le Conte de Berion, frere de mondict Seigneur de la Trimoüille.

Apres elles furent meſdames les Ducheſſes d'Aumal- . le & de Valentinois, & furent les queuës de leurs man- teaux portées,à ſçauoir de madicte Dame d'Aumale par monſeigneur le Viconte de Touraine, & de madicte Dame de Valentinois,par monſeigneur de Denuille fils de mondict Seigneur le Conneſtable.

Madamoiſelle la Baſtarde, & madame la Conneſta- ble les ſuiuyrent, portans les queuës de leurs man- teaux, à ſçauoir de madamoiſelle la Baſtarde, monſei- gneur de Chaſteauuillain, & de madicte Dame la Con- neſtable, monſeigneur de Mezieres.

Les

Les dernieres furent Madamoiſelle de Nemours, &
madame la Marquiſe du Maine, & furent les queües de
leurs manteaux portées, à ſçauoir de madiɛ̃te Damoi-
ſelle de Nemours, par monſeigneur de Rochefort de
la Rocheguyon, & de madiɛ̃te Dame la Marquiſe, par
monſeigneur de Bequincourt, fils aiſné de monſeigneur
de Humiere.

Leſdiɛ̃tes Dames, Ducheſſes & Comteſſes auoyent
leurs chapeaux & cercles de Ducheſſes & Comteſſes, &
leurs corſets & manteaux de veloux pers, & les ſurcots
d'hermines, enrichiz de pierreries, de gráde valeur, reſerué toutesfois mes Dames de Vádoſme, d'Eſtouteuille, de Montpenſier l'aiſnée, & de Valentinois veufues,
qui auoyent leurs accouſtremens ſans aucun enrichiſſement.
Apres marcha la Dame d'honneur richement veſtue.

La Royne en la compagnie que deſſus, vint à l'Egliſe, ſ'agenoüiller deuant le grand autel, ſur vn oreiller, qui
luy fut preſenté par monſeigneur de Longueuille, où
elle trouua monſeigneur le Cardinal de Bourbon reueſtu, accompaigné de monſeigneur l'Archeueſque de
Vienne Primat, & de vingtdeux Eueſques eſtans aux
deux coſtez dudit grád autel, aux lieux pour ce ordónez.

Mondit ſeigneur le Cardinal de Bourbon bailla à
baiſer à la Royne le reliquaire, diſant l'oraiſon pour ce
ordonnée: & ce faiɛ̃t fut menée ſur ledit grand eſchauf-
fauɫ eſleué de dixneuf marches deuát ledit grand autel,
& là aſſiſe en ſa chaize, poſée ſur ledit hauldez par meſ-
dits Seigneurs les Cardinaulx de Guyſe & de Van-
B ij

dofme, tenans toufiours les pans de fondict manteau, mefdicts Seigneurs les Duc de Vandofmois & Comté d'Anguyen, marchant deuant mondict feigneur le Connneftable & Grand Maiftre, qui faifoit tenir & garder l'ordre qui eftoit requis.

Apres que la Royne fut affife, madicte Dame Marguerite luy feit vne grande reuerence, & pareillement toutes les autres Princeffes & Dames, & mefmes celles qui luy portoyent la queüe, & f'affirent toutes fur les bancs preparez pour elles, chafcune en fon reng, ainfi qu'il eft cy deuant dict.

Pendant que lefdictes Dames f'affirent en leurs places, mefdicts Seigneurs les Cardinaulx de Guyfe & de Vandofme, & mefdicts Seigneurs les Duc de Vandofmois, Comte d'Anguyen, & Duc de Longueuille, defcendirent dudict grand efchauffault, & allerent à fçauoir mefdicts Seigneurs les Cardinaulx, au banc ordonné pour les Cardinaulx, & lefdicts trois Princes à l'efchauffault dreffé pour les Princes, ainfi que deffus eft recité.

Lefdicts Cardinaulx, peu de temps apres fe leuerent & retournerent fur ledict efchauffault, & femblablement mefdicts Seigneurs de Vandofme, d'Anguyen, & de Longueuille: & emmenerent lefdicts Cardinaulx ladicte Dame, deuant ledict grand autel, ayant à fes deux coftez mefdicts Seigneurs de Vandofme & d'Anguyen qui portoyent les pans de fondict manteau, & mondict Seigneur de Longueuille portant ledict oreiller deuant elle, & fut fa queüe portée par les trois Dames fufdictes.

Mondict Seigneur le Conneftable Grand Maiftre eftant toufiours deuant ladicte Dame.

Ladicte Dame paruenue deuant ledict grand autel, fe profterna faifant deuotement fon oraifon, & icelle oraifon faicte, lefdicts Cardinaulx de Guyfe & de Vādofme, la leuerent fur fes genoux, & ainfi à genoux ladicte Dame enclina fon chef pour ouÿr l'oraifon que deift mondict Seigneur le Cardinal de Bourbon.

L'oraifon par luy dicte, il print la faincte vnction, qui luy fut prefentée par Meffeigneurs les Archeuefque de Vienne Primat, & Euefque de Soyffons, C'eft à fçauoir l'Ampole, ou eftoit ladicte vnctió, par ledict Archeuefque de Vienne, & la Platine ou fut verfé icelle vnction tenoit ledict Euefque de Soyffons.

Pendant le temps que ladicte oraifon fe difoit, mondict Seigneur le Conneftable Grand Maiftre, alla querir madame Marguerite, & le Seignīr de Chemault Preuoft de l'ordre, & maiftre des ceremonies, madame la Ducheffe doüairiere de Vandofmois, & madame la Ducheffe d'Eftouteuille Comteffe de S. Pol, l'vne apres l'autre pour feruir audict Sacre.

Lefdictes trois Dames venues, mondict Seigneur le Cardinal de Bourbon print ladicte vnction, & en verfa en ladicte platine, telle quantité qu'il veit eftre neceffaire, & en oignit ladicte Dame fur fon chef, qui fut defcou uert par madicte Dame Marguerite, & apres en la poictrine qui fut defcouuerte par mefdictes Dames les Ducheffe de Vādofmois & Ducheffe d'Eftouteuille, difant

B iij

mondict Seigneur le Cardinal l'oraison pour ce ordonnée.

Ledict Cardinal procedant outre audict Sacre, print
pareillement l'Anneau qui luy fut presenté par monseigneur l'Euesque d'Eureux, & le meit au doigt de ladicte
Dame, disant aussi l'oraison sur ce ordonnée.

Ce faisant, selon l'ordre cy dessus escrit, ledict Cardinal bailla à ladicte Dame les Sceptre & main de Iustice,
lesquels luy furent presentez, sçauoir est ledict Sceptre
par monseigneur l'Euesque de Bayeux, & ladicte main
de Iustice, par monseigneur l'Euesque de Theroüenne,
& dit mondit Seigneur le Cardinal l'oraison pour ce ac-
coustumée.

Apres iceluy Cardinal print la grande Couronne qui
luy fut baillée par monsieur de Mascon grand Au-
mosnier du Roy, laquelle ledict Seigneur Cardinal pre-
senta sur le chef de ladicte Dame, sans la lascher : estant
ce pendant ladicte Courône soustenue parmondit Seigneur le Duc de Vandosmois & môdit Seigneur d'Anguyen, & depuis mise és mains de Loÿs Monsieur de
Vandosme, & au lieu d'icelle en fut posé sur la teste de
ladicte Dame par messeigneurs de Vandosme & d'Anguyen vne autre petite toute couuerte & enrichie de
dyamans, rubiz, & perles de grandissime pris & excelléce. Et en ce faisant ladicte Dame se deschargea dudict
Sceptre és mains de monseigneur le Duc de Montpensier, & de la main de Iustice és mains de monseigneur le
Prince de la Roche sur-Yon.

Ledict Sacre faict, & oraisons dictes par môdict Sei-

gneur le Cardinal de Bourbon, la Royne fut remenée
par mefdicts Seigneurs les Cardinaux en fa chaize fur
ledict haudez, & marchoyent deuant elle lefdicts Seigneurs de Montpenfier & Prince de la Roche-Suryon
auec ledict Sceptre & main de Iuftice, & deuãt eux Loÿs
monfieur de Vandofme tenant efleuée ladicte grande
Couronne, dont ladicte Dame auoit efté Couronnée :
mondict feigneur de Longueuille portant l'oreiller deuant & marchant en ceft ordre depuis ledict grand autel
iufques fur ledict hauldez. Mefdicts feigneurs de Vandofme & d'Anguyen tindrent les deux coftez de fon
mãteau, & alloit deuant ladicte Dame mõdict Seigneur
le Conneftable grand maiftre.

Ladicte Dame eftant affife ainfi pour ouïr meffe, lefdicts Cardinaux f'en retournerent feoir en leur fiege, &
Loÿs monfieur de Vandofme pofa deuant elle fur vn
efcabeau à ce ordonné couuert de veloux pers, femé de
fleurs de lis ladicte grande Couronne, & fe tint ledict
Prince à genoux pres ledict efcabeau.

Aux deux coftez de ladicte Dame eftoyét auffi à genoux meffeigneurs les Duc de Montpenfier, & Prince
de la Rochefuryon : mondit feigneur de Montpenfier
tenant le Sceptre à main droicte, & mondit feigneur le
Prince de la Rochefuryon fon frere ladicte main de Iuftice à main feneftre.

Ladicte Dame ainfi affife en fa chaize que dit eft, mefdits feigneurs les Duc de Vandofmois & Comte d'An
guyen demourerent continuellement ioingnant elle
d'vn cofté & d'autre faifant contenance de luy aider à
fouftenir la Couronne qui eftoit fur fon chef.

Et lors fe commença à celebrer la meſſe par mondict ſeigneur le Cardinal de Bourbon, qui fut dicte à deux diacres & deux ſoubs diacres. Leſdicts diacres furent l'Eueſque de Chartres chantant, & l'Eueſque de Rennes aſſiſtant: & deit l'Euangile ledict Eueſque de Chartres. Les ſoubs diacres furent monſeigneur l'Eueſque de Sees chantant, qui deit l'Epiſtre, & monſeigneur l'Eueſque de Ciſteron aſſiſtant.

Au commencemēt de ladicte meſſe la Dame d'honneur preſenta à madamoiſelle la Baſtarde les heures de la Royne, & à madame la Conneſtable vn liure d'oraiſons, qui l'vne apres l'autre les preſenterent à ladicte Dame, & puis ſen retournerent aſſeoir en leurs places.

Et quant ſe vint à dire l'Euangile, mondict Seigneur le Cardinal de Bourbon donna la benediction à monſeigneur l'Eueſque de Chartres qui deit ledict Euangile, & apres preſenta le liure à monſeigneur le Cardinal de Boullongne, lequel accompagné deſdits deux diacres alla trouuer ladicte Dame, & ayant pris de mondict Seigneur l'Eueſque de Chartres au hault dudict eſchaufault ledict liure, bailla à baiſer à ladicte Dame l'Euangile, laquelle pour ce faire, ſagenoüilla ſur l'oreiller qui auoit eſté poſé & laiſſé deuant elle par mondict Seigneur de Longueuille, ſeſtant ladicte Dame tenue debout au parauant durant iceluy Euangile, & pareillement toutes les autres dames apres luy auoir fait vne grande reuerence.

Durant auſſi ledict Euangile ſe tindrent debout meſdicts Seigneurs de Vandoſme & d'Anguyen, & pareillement

lement mefdits feigneurs les Ducs de Montpenfier &
Prince de la Rochefuryon auec ledit Sceptre & main de
Iuftice,& femblablement Loÿs monfieur de Vandofme
tenant en fes mains efleuée ladiéte grande Couronne
qu'il auoit au parauant pofée fur ledit petit efcabeau.

Apres ledit Euangile fini & le Credo dit,les trois Dames ordónées pour porter à ladiéte Dame d'honneur le
pain,le vin, le cierge auec l'argét pour offrir eftás en leur
petit efchauffault bas,cy deffus declairé, qui furent mes
Dames la Marefchalle de faiét André,la Seignore Siluia
fille de mófeigneur le Cóte de Lamirádolle, & madame
la Cóteffe de faiét Aignan. Ayás receu lefdiétes offertes
par les mains dudit feigneur de Chemault Preuoft de
l'ordre,& maiftre des ceremonies, móterent l'vne apres
l'autre fur ledit grand efchauffault. Premierement ma-
diéte dame la Marefchalle de faiét André auec les deux
pains,l'vn doré & l'autre argenté. Apres elle la Seignore
Siluia auecques le vin, & la troifieme la Conteffe de S.
Aignan auec vn cierge de cire vierge, auquel eftoyent
attachées treze pieces d'or : & à mefure qu'elles mon-
toyent, apres auoir fait deux grandes reuerences à l'entrée dudit grand efchauffault, l'vne vers le grand autel,
& l'autre vers la Royne,baillerét à ladiéte Dame d'honneur lefdiétes offertes qui les prefenta à mefure qu'elle
les receut,fçauoir eft le pain qui eftoit doré à madame la
Ducheffe de Guyfe, l'autre pain qui eftoit argenté à madame la Ducheffe de Niuernois la ieune, le vin à madame la Ducheffe d'Aumalle,& le cierge auquel eftoyent
attachées lefdits treze pieces d'or à madame de Valentinois.

Et lors partant ladiéte Dame pour aller à l'offerte, fe

leuerent de rechef toutes lefdictes dames, & luy feirent
vne grande reuerence, & l'accompaignerent mefdits feigneurs les Cardinaux de Guyfe & de Vandofme, & les
quatre Dames à qui furent baillées lefdictes offertes, qui
l'vne apres l'autre les luy prefenterent à l'autel, luy portant auffi la queüe les autres dames à ce ordonnées: mefdits feigneurs les Duc de Vandofmois & Conte d'Anguyen tenans toufiours les deux pans de fondit mâteau,
& mefdits feigneurs les Duc de Montpenfier & Prince
de la Rochefuryon allans deuant auec lefdits Sceptre &
main de Iuftice, Loÿs monfieur de Vandofme auec ladicte grande Couronne, & mondit feigneur de Longueuille portant deuant ledit oreiller, marchant pareillemẽt
mondit feigneur le Conneftable Grandmaiftre deuant
ladicte Dame.

Ladicte offerte faicte, ladicte Dame retourna f'afleoir
en fa chaize accompagnée cõme deffus, & quãd ce vint
à la leuatiõ du *corpus Domini*, elle fe leua de fadicte chaize
pour f'agenoüiller, & pareillement madame Marguerit-
te, & les autres Princeffes & Dames qui luy feirent vne
autre grande reuerence. Mefdits feigneurs les Duc de
Vandofmois & Conte d'Anguyen toufiours à cofté
d'elle, & mefdits feigneurs les Duc de Montpenfier &
Prince de la Rochefuryon tenans lefdits Sceptre &
main de Iuftice, & pareillement Loÿs monfieur de Vandofme ladicte grande Couronne efleuée en fes mains
durant l'eleuation dudit *corpus Domini*.

Apres ladicte eleuation & benediction dicte par mõdit feigneur le Cardinal de Bourbon, quand ce vint à
l'Agnus Dei, mondit feigneur le Cardinal de Boullongne
alla baifer monfeigneur le Cardinal de Bourbon offi-
ciant,

ciant,& depuis ladicte Dame à la iouë en figne de paix,
laquelle f'agenoüilla de rechef fur fon deffufdit oreiller, qui luy fut prefenté par mondit feigneur de Longueuille.

Apres ledit *Agnus Dei* & confommation faicte du *corpus Domini* par mondit feigneur le Cardinal de Bourbon, ladicte Dame fut amenée de rechef audit grand
Autel par mefdits feigneurs les Cardinaux de Guyfe &
de Vandofme, ayant auec elle mefdits feigneurs les Duc
de Vandofmois & Conte d'Anguyen qui portoyent les
pans de fondit manteau, & les fufdictes trois Dames la
queuë, marchans auffi les Princes qui portoyent lefdits
Sceptre, main de Iuftice, grande Couronne, & oreiller,
& là elle receut en grande reuerence & deuotion le *corpus Domini* par les mains de mondit feigneur le Cardinal
de Bourbon, & apres auoir fait fon oraifon, f'en retourna fur ladicte chaize en la compagnie que deffus, où elle
acheua d'ouŷr ladicte meffe.

La Meffe dicte & acheuée la Royne defcendit en l'ordre que deffus marchans deuant elle mefdits feigneurs
les Ducs de Montpenfier & Prince de la Rochefuryon
auec ledit Sceptre & main de Iuftice, Loÿs monfieur de
Vandofme auec ladicte grande Couronne.

Et lors mondit feigneur le Duc de Vãdofmois la print
par deffoubs le bras droit, & mõdit feigneur d'Anguyen
par deffoubs le gauche, & meffeigneurs les Ducs de
Guyfe & de Nemours que l'on auoit fait defcendre de
l'efchauffault des Princes où ils auoyent efté durant le
feruice, prindrent les pans de fondit manteau, que tenoyent au parauant mefdits Seigneurs : & ainfi accompagnée defdictes Dames, Princes & Seigneurs cy deuant
nommez, la remenerent en fa chambre.

Et fault entendre que durant la celebration defdits Sacre & Couronnement, les queuës ne furent portées aux Princeffes & Dames qui y feruirent, & n'y auoit fur ledit grand efchauffault que les deffufdictes Dames affifes en leurs lieux comme dict eft, & lefdits Princes qui y feruirent auec les feigneurs & gentils-hommes qui porterent les queuës defdictes Dames quand elles entrerent & fortirent de l'Eglife, qui fe tindrent derriere elles fans faire aucun empefchement, & pareillement mófeigneur le Conneftable ayant l'œil & regard à tout, & ledit de Chemault auec luy, auquel il ordonnoit ce qui eftoit à faire pour accomplir les ceremonies.

Fault auffi noter que monfeigneur de Lorges Cheualier de l'ordre, Capitaine de la garde Efcoffoife, & les feigneurs de Chauigny, Deftrée, & la Ferté, Capitaines des trois bendes de la garde Françoife, eftoyent partie fur le bas efchauffault dreffé deffoubs celuy des Princes comme dict eft cy deuant, & partie au dedans du cueur auec quelque nombre d'archers pour garder qu'il n'y euft aucun defordre audit facre & couronnement.

A la fin de ladicte Meffe fut criée l'argeffe de par ladicte Dame au dedans de l'Eglife par vn des heraux d'armes d'vne bonne fomme d'or & d'argent qui fut iettée au peuple par le treforier de ladicte Dame à diuerfes fois.

Les Ambaffadeurs refidens pres la perfonne du Roy qui fe trouuerent audit Sacre & Couronnement, furent l'Ambaffadeur du Pape, celuy de l'Empereur, celuy de Angleterre, celuy d'Efcoffe, les deux Ambaffadeurs de la Seigneurie de Venife, & celuy de Ferrare.

F I N.

The Entry of Henri II Into Paris, 1549 includes the facsimile of both the *livret* of the royal entry and of the Queen's *Sacre*, which was published as a companion to the main entry. Based on manuscript material in the Archives Nationales and on published sources, the substantial introduction deals with the circumstances in which the Entry belatedly took place, considers its artistic relationship to other ceremonies of the time, and places it in the context of the Neo-classical aesthetic emerging in France at the time of the Pleiade's beginnings. Architectural matters, literary sources, mythography, and literary aspects of the *livret* are surveyed. Appended to the introduction is a detailed bibliography of primary sources and useful secondary sources.

I. D. McFarlane is the Professor of French at Oxford University, Fellow of Wadham College, and Fellow of the British Academy. His books and articles include *Maurice Scève: Délie* (1966); *Renaissance France 1470–1589* (1974); essays in *Age of the Renaissance* (1967) and in *Ronsard the Poet* (1973); and studies on Jean Salmon Macrin, Paul Bourget, and George Buchanan. A major book on Buchanan is forthcoming.

m R t s

medieval & Renaissance texts & studies
is the publishing program of the
Center for Medieval and Early Renaissance Studies
at the State University of New York at Binghamton.

mRts aims to provide the highest quality scholarship
in attractive and durable format at modest cost.